Last Freedom

Short Plays by Robin Wyatt Dunn

Weasel Press
Hitching for Words

Author: Robin Wyatt Dunn
Title: Last Freedom

ISBN-10: 0692350985
ISBN-13: 978-0692350980
Library of Congress Number: 2015940304

© 2015 Robin Wyatt Dunn
www.robindunn.com

Published through Weasel Press
Located in Manvel, TX
http://www.weaselpress.com
http://www.facebook.com/weaselpress

ALL RIGHTS RESERVED. This book contains material protected under International and Federal Copyright Laws and Treaties. Any unauthorized reprint or use of this material is prohibited. No part of this book, or use of characters in this book, may be reproduced or transmitted in any form or by any means, electronic or mechanical, including photocopying, recording, or by any information storage and retrieval system without express written permission from the author / publisher.

Table of Contents

Calvin & Hobbes............................5

Spirit Journey.............................50

Dubya Operetta..........................56

The Jump....................................71

Two Jews....................................76

A Man Stands...........................124

A Marriage Play.......................133

I Am Chumash, I Am Aching...163

For Brad Friedman

Hobbes & Calvin

Scene 1

Julia delivers the following while undressing, being videotaped.

So this could be my last moment of freedom? I've thought about this for a really long time. To be a possession. To be possessed. Why did they give it to you? Don't do it yet, okay? You have to warn me. I hope it doesn't hurt too much. But I want it to hurt, at least a little. It should hurt, to become a slave. Albemuth . . .

What will I feel? Will it be what you want me to feel? Will it be like I'm dreaming? Be gentle with me.

Scene 2

The same room, later. Hobbes and Calvin are talking.

H: I don't see what your point is: are you suggesting we make art?

C: No. Not that.

H: You say, "go to the people, let them decide." Sounds great. What would that mean?

C: I don't know.

H: You do know.

C: No.

H: Yes.

C: What time is it?

H: 2, maybe.

C: Are you going to sign the contract?

H: I don't know.

C: Why wouldn't you?

H: Are you?

C: No.

H: You're not?

C: No.

H: Why not?

C: As a statement.

H: Fat lot of good that'll do you. Probably get us both jail terms.

C: No. They won't send us to jail.

H: They could.

C: You're romanticizing.

H: Jail isn't romantic.

C: Let's go over it again.

H: Okay.

C: You walk into the plaza, outside the subway.

H: And I announce: "I am Dr. Pepper!"

C: And I say: "I am Coca-Cola!"

H: You must decide which of us is best!

C: Taste us!

H: Enjoy us!

C: We are beverages made for you!

H: We could have maybe 25 minutes before the cops show up — so we have to keep the audience going till then.

C: I'm not sure I want to go outside today.

H: Sure you do. It's a nice day.

C: Yes.

H: It is.

C: Yes.

H: Do you believe in the future of our country?

C: You mean: do I think it'll be good? Good for who? For us? For the rich it'll be fine; it's always fine for the rich. For a while. Things change. You can't predict the future.

H: We're in this swamp, this great American swamp, now.

C: Politics.

H: Save me, save me.

C: I'll save you.

H: Will you?

C: Why should I?

H: I want to be saved.

C: Do you? Why? You don't believe in the future. Why do you want to be in it?

H: I want to be in it.

C: Do you? Prove it.

H: You called McDonald's, didn't you?

C: Yes.

H: Oh God.

C: Prove that you want to be in our future.

H: I will be anyway, won't I? What will it mean? To be "in it"?

C: Open minded. It would mean that. You see, you're not open minded enough!

H: Aren't I?

C: No, you're not.

H: Could I be?

C: Could you?

H: Yes.

C: I didn't call McDonald's.

H: You called Burger King then.

C: No.

H: Jack in the Box.

C: No.

H: In and Out.

C: No. I didn't call anyone.

H: You did.

C: They called me.

H: What did you say?

C: I said I was for sale.

H: Were those your exact words?

C: No, not exactly.

H: What were your exact words to the corporation in question?

C: I don't remember.

H: What were your approximate words.

C: I was crying.

Hobbes goes to the closet and opens it and peers inside.

H: What are you going to do with her?

C: I don't know.

H: How old is she?

C: 22, maybe.

H: Did you rape her?

C: Of course not.

H: Good. That's good. She's asleep.

Hobbes closes the closet door.

H: Where did you find her?

C: By the subway.

H: By the subway.

C: Yes.

H: What will you do with her?

C: I don't know.

H: Does she trust you?

C: She did for a minute.

H: I don't suppose it matters now.

C: It matters.

H: Yes, but not as much. You've kidnapped her now. You're a felon.

C: I didn't kidnap her, exactly.

H: Yes you did. She's tied up in your closet.

C: She came of her own free will.

H: Well, she's your prisoner now, anyway.

C: Yes. I won't hurt her. You know that.

H: You've hurt her already. What will you do with her?

C: Nothing too drastic. She's very pretty. She'll be useful. We'll make a video or something. Have her read the statement to the government.

H: Ridiculous.

C: It'll get us noticed.

H: You've already been noticed.

C: You too.

H: Not really. I've gotten better at not being noticed. I've even been paid for that.

C: What will you do when I'm gone?

H: I'll manage.

C: Will you?

H: Yes.

C: Without me to assuage your fears?

Hobbes laughs.

C: You'll be fine, probably.

H: Yes.

C: Tell me what McDonald's said to you.

H: It wasn't McDonald's.

C: Coca-Cola then.

H: The corporation, which shall remain nameless, told me they had seen my resume, and wondered if I was free for an interview.

C: Uh huh.

H: The woman was very nice. Early 30s probably. A sweet, rather uninflected voice. A dead voice, really. A woman who never had to think too hard.

C: Yes.

H: I felt like throwing myself in front of a bus, then. Just hearing her voice. Mostly because she was so hypnotic. Suddenly I wanted to live in her world! I wanted health insurance again! I wanted a car, and new toothpaste, and a lawn. God, a lawn, that you mow, or hire someone to mow.

C: What did she ask you?

H: About my employment history.

C: What did you tell her?

H: I told her I was a therapist.

Calvin laughs.

C: That's a good one! I like that!

H: Yes, I thought you'd like that one.

C: Is it true?

H: Is what true?

C: That Albemuth really is orbiting?

H: I don't know.

C: You know something.

H: Not really.

C: You do.

H: If I did, I wouldn't necessarily tell you, would I?

C: Tell me.

H: No.

Calvin gets up and tries to pace the tiny room and isn't very successful in doing so.

H: How long are you going to leave her in there?

C: She's asleep.

H: Not for long.

C: For a while yet.

H: What did you give her?

C: Just some aspirin, that's all.

H: Aspirin, huh?

C: I offered her whiskey too. She didn't want it.

H: How generous of you. How does it feel, being a kidnapper?

C: Strange.

H: Don't you feel omnipotent? You could do whatever you wanted to her.

C: I feel weaker. Decisions, decisions.

H: Decisions, decisions.

C: I need to take a nap.

H: You can't nap now.

C: Why don't you take a walk or something.

H: Now?

C: If you like.

H: Albemuth is orbiting above us.

C: Let us be saved. Let us be rearranged. Let God come down via satellite and free us from care and worry, let his face be revealed.

H: Yes, yes.

C: Let Albemuth be won, let Albemuth be lost, let us assuage ourselves in the rich peat moss, sinking down to die . . .

H: Poets are so dangerous, aren't they.

C: Only armed poets.

H: Are you armed?

C: I was 5150'd, remember? Illegal for me to buy weapons.

H: But you could get them anyway, if you wanted.

C: I suppose. Make friends with gangsters.

H: Like me.

C: Not your kind of gangster. The old fashioned kind that likes poor alleyways.

H: Yes. There's a poor alleyway behind your building.

C: Anyway. So it's Stars Wars at last!

H: Reagan would be so proud.

C: All you have to do is make a call.

H: In theory.

C: Isn't that what they told you?

H: Not exactly.

C: Isn't that what they always tell you?

H: You are a paranoid son of a bitch, aren't you.

C: Well, you know what Woody Allen said about it.

H: "Just because you're paranoid, doesn't mean they're not out to get you!"

C: So you want the lawn? The health insurance? Is that why you said yes?

H: I didn't say yes.

C: Yes you did. Of course you did.

H: I want a wife.

C: Ah.

H: Is that so surprising?

C: No.

H: If I am loyal, I will be granted the right to a woman.

C: Very simple, isn't it. Like Mormonism!

H: You have your own methods, of course. Tie them up in your closet!

Calvin laughs.

H: You could still let her go. She might not even report you.

C: Of course she would.

H: I could help you kill her.

C: What would that accomplish?

H: Well, she couldn't report you then.

C: Then we'd be murderers. Besides, I don't want to kill her. She's an innocent.

H: How innocent is she?

C: Innocent enough.

H: Do you think she believes in the Albemuth satellite?

C: She may believe the official version.

H: She probably does. It's even true, is the funny part.

C: Yes, it does contain a radio telescope, doesn't it.

H: Yes, it's just not especially interested in the stars.

C: Who do you call? To make it work?

H: Don't you want to get married?

C: Do you call their Public Relations Department? Department of Mind Control?

H: You're a beautiful innocent.

C: I don't think I know you anymore.

H: But you do know me.

C: My tiger friend.

H: (*grinning*) Yes. Calvin, why don't you go and lie down next to your woman for a minute.

C: She's not my woman.

H: Well she's yours for the time being, isn't she? Why don't you go and get a good smell of her. Spoon with her. Hold her. Smell her skin and her hair.

C: Only you can decide, which sugarly love beverage is for you! Mr. Pibb or Mountain Dew! Green gold or caramel wine? We're both fizzy, and we're both available near you!

H: You should do it. It would do you good. Remind you why you haven't hurt her. Why you haven't torn up the contract.

C: Involuntary servitude is illegal in this country.

H: Is it?

C: Are you hungry?

H: Hungry?

C: Yes. Are you?

H: Do you ever use this hulking monster? (*pointing at desktop computer monitors*)

C: Not much anymore.

H: It's your film editing machine?

C: It was.

H: Why not sell it, if you don't use it?

C: Nostalgia.

H: That's why you came to the city?

C: Yes.

H: A shame.

C: Not really.

H: It is, though.

C: You're the shame.

H: You were just another rat listening to our pan pipes.

C: You listened too.

H: If you're hungry, eat.

C: She might be hungry.

H: She's sleeping, let her be.

C: Why did you sign?

H: You could make films again, if you had sponsorship. It's no different from patronage. It worked for James Joyce.

C: Joyce lived in the pre- mind control satellite era.

H: They don't like to use it, you know.

C: Oh no.

H: It's very expensive.

C: How expensive is it?

H: Very expensive.

C: In more ways than one.

H: How much better to have you sign willingly! In the long run.

C: Yes, what a coup for them. Coke is it. Join with Sauron, or move to the Spice Islands.

H: I vote for the latter!

C: Do you know why I brought her?

H: For sex?

C: Partly. To feel her close by. To know there is a woman in my closet, right behind the door. Right there, right behind the door, a woman, a young beautiful woman, who

I chose, who I delivered to myself, who I gave to myself, who I seduced.

H: Did you seduce her?

C: Yes.

H: How did you seduce her?

C: With power.

H: Tell me.

C: With memory.

H: Yes?

C: With promises of love.

H: Ahhhh.

C: I knew she wanted meaning. Meaning. Like syllable from sound, meaning, to be held, to be wanted, to be transgressed and plucked, plucked from a rut into a drama. Drama, drama, drama, from safety into peril under the eyes of a watchful man. To watch her, you see, that's what I wanted. Without interruption.

H: Sounds kinky.

C: Haven't you ever felt that way?

Pause.

C: I wanted to record her. Not just with my camera but

with my mind, to remember her. To remember her when she was young, and when I was young too, whether I'm young or not anymore I don't know, but I wanted to feel young in remembering her, to watch her and see her seeing me watch her, to know she wanted exactly that, to slip into the oldest dream of all, a rape. Like Persephone and the Sabine Women.

H: You did rape her then.

C: I abducted her.

H: But she followed of her own free will.

C: Perhaps I mind controlled her.

H: You haven't signed the contract.

C: What would my contractual obligations be?

H: Whatever they wanted them to be.

C: What are yours?

H: I haven't signed yet.

C: You're distracting me.

H: That's my job.

C: I saw her and I knew. Fire, fire, slumbering in her eyes, the knowledge that comes alive only in submission, in weakness, she wanted to be weak, you see, so she could be strong. She wanted to remember, too. She wanted to remember that pain of her ancestors, to know the headache and the disillusion, the majestic evil of surrender to a man who holds you in thrall. In thrall, enthrall, in thrall.

H: Maybe we'll stamp out the poets, eh?

C: Yes, lazy buggers.

H: We could make her dance.

C: She's sleeping. You don't really believe in Albemuth do you?

H: Of course I do.

C: You really believe you can make a phone call and make some satellite control me like a little puppet?

H: You want to try it?

Hobbes takes out his phone.

C: Not just yet. I need a nap is what I need. Aren't you tired?

H: Didn't you sleep last night?

C: Not well.

H: Guilty conscience?

C: Where did Albemuth come from?

H: We made it. Like Sputnick.

C: Did we?

H: Sure we did.

C: How do you know?

H: I don't. It's just what I think. Where do you think Albemuth came from?

C: Aliens.

H: But what is an alien?

C: Illegal aliens.

H: Won't you sign the contract? If you marry, we can be neighbors again. I'd like that.

C: But we're neighbors now.

H: Not for much longer. When twilight comes I'll be gone, and so will you, and so will she.

C: That soon?

H: Yes.

C: Why?

H: The free market is swift to react!

Calvin laughs.

H: Albemuth is just an overflow valve, you see? Who really wants zombie slaves all the time? You're much more efficient as semi-autonomous processors of information.

C: Who is?

H: Human beings. Free human beings.

C: You've been spending time with their marketing group.

H: You should too. It would give you some good ideas.

C: Hobbes, are you still my tiger friend?

H: Of course.

C: Till the end?

H: Naturally.

C: But the end is soon now, isn't it.

H: Sooner.

C: Let's review again. I step into the plaza, spread my arms wide, and announce:
I am Coca-Cola, I am brown and fizzy! I am manufactured in America! And Mexico! Sugar fills me for your good! I am brown and fizzy!

H: And I am Mountain Dew! I am green and sexy! I am filled with caffeinated goodness! Do me, I am the Dew! I am your friend!

C: I live love and prosper in your mouth and in your belly! I am sound and safe in your lips! I am a stimulating afternoon, a warm summer day! I am the ephemeral dream of your summery America! I come to you! I come to you for your salvation! No longer is the cane worked by slaves in

South America, no longer do we trade them for our rum, our brown is only caramel color! We richen you, we live for you, we brew in the stainless steel disinfected vats in Texas and we sing your anthems and surprises! Happy Birthday, just for you! I am Coca-Cola and I serve! I serve you, son! Would you like some ice!

H: I am green and mighty! Green like the currency of your former nation! Green like a mountain stream! Green like a wondrous algae bloom! Green like the message into the dark that is our life on Earth, our wondrous life! Drink me, and drink me true, I am the Dew! I am the morning Mountain Dew! I collect on blades of grass, and on your daughter's face, sleeping soundly on the mountain side upon her pad of polycarbonate, upon her first decade of life, I settle down into her bones for freedom and for victory, for a tricentennial of revolution . . .

C: And who is best! You must decide!

Pause.

H: It's a good shtick.

C: Yes.

H: What will you do with the woman?

C: Free her.

H: But she doesn't want to be free.

C: Yes she does.

H: Are you sure?

C: Yes.

H: She doesn't understand what freedom is.

C: And you do?

H: You should rest. I'll watch her while you sleep.

C: What is mind control anyway?

H: You just shoot someone with The Ray.

C: And then what?

H: Then you give orders to the satellite.

C: What kind of orders?

H: Any kind.

C: You can't just give me orders?

H: Perhaps it's only a metaphor.

C: Albemuth is real. Like Radio Free Europe was real.

H: Yes, perhaps.

C: I've seen it.

H: Seen what?

C: The satellite. Through my friend's telescope.

H: What friend?

C: I saw it. He showed me.

H: But what did you really see?

C: I don't understand. What's the point?

H: Fear is the point. It's subtle, but it's real. Did we ever acquire a technology we didn't use? It's the using that makes it a technology. Knowledge doesn't exist in a vacuum. It's a tool. Tools are made by using them.

C: You are wise, grasshopper.

H: I'm tired. Like you.

C: Yes.

H: Do you love the woman?

C: The woman in the closet?

H: What's her name?

C: Julia.

H: Julia. Like Juliette.

C: Yes.

H: Do you love her?

C: Yes.

H: You do?

C: Yes.

H: Why?

C: She's beautiful.

H: You didn't tell me that part.

Hobbes gets up, opens closet again, looks inside.

H: She is beautiful, isn't she?

C: She's an American woman.

Hobbes closes the closet, sits back down.

H: Yes.

C: What do you think it means?

H: Her being an American?

C: Yes.

H: What do you think it means?

C: She's wise. She's stuck. Between the Aztecs and the Spanish; between the Puritans and the Anarchists. She can be neither one; she must be both woman and lady, both woman and lady, and accept the weaknesses of both.

H: You sympathize with her.

C: Of course I do. I've got her tied up in my closet.

H: Why not let her go?

C: Should I?

H: You're asking me?

C: What if I do let her go?

H: Why did she come to you in the first place?

C: She was lonely. She wanted to be less lonely.

H: But why you?

C: I don't know.

H: Why do you think she did?

C: She liked what I promised her. The surrender. The life of someone slipping away, heroin without the needles. Freedom.

H: You offered her freedom.

C: Yes.

H: You offered her Radio Free Albemuth.

C: Please don't mention that book.

H: It's not a book.

C: Yes, it's a book.

H: No, it isn't.

C: What is it then?

H: Who are you?

C: I'm Calvin. I am the boy Calvin. I am Calvin. I live in America. I am only a man!

H: You are a man, aren't you.

C: And you're Hobbes. You're a tiger, Hobbes. A tiger.

H: I know, yes. How much radio did you give her?

C: Only a few minutes.

H: She'd never gotten a dose of it before?

C: Not Albemuth, no.

H: Why did you give it to her?

C: She wanted it.

H: Do you believe Albemuth is a satellite?

C: What else could it be?

H: It matters what it is. For instance, if it's more local — a microwave dish somewhere in our fair city, for instance, it could very well be a local subsidiary transmitting the Albemuth signal. It might even originate here, on Earth. How can we know it's in orbit?

C: I don't know. Because it feels alien.

H: Yes. But what does that mean— feeling alien.

C: When did you sign, Hobbes? When did you sign the loyalty oath?

H: I didn't sign.

C: You did.

H: I didn't. I swear.

C: I don't believe you.

H: Why would I sign? What would I gain?

C: Everything. A woman. Money. A job. A life, here in the city.

H: We still believe in hard work in America.

C: Do we?

H: I do. Let's get out of here, take a walk.

C: No.

H: Aren't you getting claustrophobic?

C: No. We're getting somewhere. How long have we been talking?

H: All afternoon?

C: It is you talking isn't it?

H: Yes.

C: You are the one controlling your own mouth? You're not a zombie?

H: You mean, how can you know I'm not a zombie? You can never know that.

C: It's too paranoid, you're right. Let's have a drink or something.

H: You shouldn't drink alcohol, not in your condition.

C: You're probably right. I'm just afraid, though, just afraid.

H: Liquid courage doesn't make fear go away. You need to be strong. Be strong.

C: I know. Help me, Hobbes.

H: I'm trying, buddy. Sign the contract, that's the first step. Here.

Hobbes hands Calvin a blank piece of paper.

C: Sign the blank piece of paper, right.

H: And they fill out the rest. You know how things work in this town. Trust is everything. The contract is only a symbol of that trust.

C: I know.

H: So sign it. Make everything easier. You could even

keep the girl.

C: The woman.

H: The woman, yes.

C: I could, couldn't I?

Hobbes laughs.

H: You know better than that.

C: Which woman do I want?

H: The free woman in a slave society, or the slave woman in a free society?

C: Semantics.

H: Semantics are important. Semantics is meaning. What do you want your woman to mean?

C: Aside from children?

H: In addition to children. In addition to love.

C: What else is there.

H: Meaning.

C: Do you want her?

H: You're the one tied her up in your closet.

C: Will I go to prison?

H: Probably.

C: Even if I release her now?

H: It's not about her, it's about you. What. Are you. Going to do. Now.

C: I don't know, I don't know!

H: You do know.

C: Call the satellite.

Silence. Long pause. They look at each other.

H: Not yet.

C: Go on, call it. Mr. Big Shot. Mr. Mow My Own Lawn. Call Albemuth.

Pause.

H: It's best I don't.

C: Do you think Philip K. Dick knew about Albemuth back in the 70s when he wrote the book?

H: I don't know. I suppose he did. Or maybe they just modeled it after his book. That seems more likely to me. Like Reagan called his anti missile plan Star Wars.

C: She really wanted it. I gave her just a little dose. Just a little transistor for a few minutes.

H: You can still decide to die painlessly. We can do that for you.

C: Now it's we again. Which we now, Hobbes?

H: The corporation which shall remain nameless.

C: Dupont? Monsanto? GE?

H: A conglomerate.

C: They're all conglomerates.

H: It's not important. What is important is you're important to us, Calvin. We want to bring you in, bring you in to the team. Don't stay out in the cold, you came this far, you knew there was no going back. Come on.

C: But I didn't know. I didn't know what it meant.

H: You knew enough. You were old enough. You asked questions and you got them answered and you didn't like the answers you got, so what. Happens to everyone. So now: what do you do with the knowledge you have?

C: I don't know.

H: Well, let me help you out here. You've got 3 options. One, sign the contract, come work with me. Keep the girl, accept reasonable limits on your behavior, live the American Dream. Option One is a nice option. Option Two: I'll give you my gun, and you blow your brains out. It's a Magnum 45, it'll do the job fine. I'll get someone to clean up the mess, you'll have a nice closed casket funeral, everyone'll be there, game over. Option Two sucks. Option 3: you don't sign the contract. I take the girl away. I

take away this little apartment. I take away your passport.
I delete all records of your name. I make things very unpleasant for you here in America. You're alive, but you're
a crazy homeless person ranting about mind control satellites. You never get laid again. How do you like Option 3?

C: I think you should leave.

H: You think I should leave?

C: I don't want you here.

Hobbes laughs uproariously.

H: Come on, be serious. I just laid it out for you.

C: I'm serious.

H: Shit, Calvin is serious?

Hobbes stands up.

H: You're serious?

C: You're still my tiger friend.

H: Of course I am! Let me help you! Let me help you, man!

C: Help me by leaving. Just go. Just get out. Go, if you're my friend, go.

H: But I can't. I'm in an impossible situation, buddy. What are friends for if not to keep you from doing something stupid? Shit, this is basically a one-man intervention.

I mean, I wish I'd brought your mom and cousins and stuff and we could read our loving statements of support for you and your decision to end chemical dependency, but I guess I'm kind of the pusher here, aren't I. Our signal is a beautiful, beautiful drug, Calvin mon frère. It is really beautiful. It crosses that blood/brain barrier, and wham, you are in control. You are powerful. You are in the room.

C: In the room.

H: Yeah. You know that's what it's like.

C: Yeah. In that special room.

H: Fuck what you call it! I want to live, don't you?

C: Of course I do!

H: Then just sign! Be like the Sephardic Jews who didn't flee! Convert but it doesn't mean shit! Because you cannot flee, man. Just sign now and it'll still be okay! I'd love you for doing that, man! Just be strong for me! Then we'll go get drunk off our asses, okay?

Hobbes sits down next to Calvin, puts his arm around him.

H: I love you, man. Do it for me. Just sign the paper.

Long pause.

C: I'll sign it. Later, okay? Not right now?

H: Okay. Okay.

Hobbes sighs, stands up and paces a little.

C: You still want to do The Coca Cola Mountain Dew routine?

H: They'll probably let us!

C: Right.

H: It's good comedy!

C: Yeah.

H: I mean, they're more likely to put it on the shelf, get someone more famous to play the parts, you know? But we'd get paid pretty well!

C: Right. That sucks.

H: We could still do it live, maybe. They might like that, too. I don't know, to tell you the truth.

C: Well, what do you think?

H: I think it's still better to ask for forgiveness than permission.

C: Yeah.

Calvin smiles.

H: There's that smile. I've been waiting for that smile!

Calvin laughs a little.

H: You've got a handsome smile, Calvin.

C: Thanks.

H: Let me tell you a story. About how I found out about it. I was down in Mexico. Down in Ensenada, all the rich gringos and some poor ones like me hanging out, drinking tequila in a café, those cafes are getting expensive, you know? And this woman comes up to me, this beautiful little chica, brown skin, beautiful smile, an ass I just want to shove my face into. An ass that makes you thank God a little for making. I ask her, what's the difference between sex and love? She tells me her opinion. I listen. I liked watching her think. Watching her eyes move, her tits sway in the Mexican sun. She threw the oysters back out to the beach, to make new oysters. When she looked back, her eyes were different. She had different eyes. You know we're dreaming here, don't you, buddy? Are you ready to wake up?

C: Oh fuck.

H: Are you ready to wake up?

C: Fuck. Fuck fuck fuck fuck fuck fuck fuck fuck . . .

H: I love you, Calvin. We all love you so much. We love you so much, Calvin. You are so fucking strong. You're too strong, don't you know that? You undertand that part. You have to be strong with us. Be strong with us, Calvin. That's what men do, Calvin. They pick sides, Calvin. They pick sides. No man is alone, Calvin! We are not alone!

Calvin signs the paper. He starts laughing, and crying. Hobbes embraces him.

H: (*While embracing*) You did good, buddy. You did so good.

Hobbes releases Calvin from his embrace.

H: Let's have a drink, huh?

C: Okay.

H: You got something to drink?

C: No.

H: Shit. I forget how broke you are.

C: Yeah. Sorry.

Hobbes picks up the paper Calvin signed, folds it, puts it in his jacket pocket.

H: I'll take care of things.

C: Yeah.

H: We're gonna be rich, man.

C: Yeah.

H: You're loyal!

C: Yep.

H: And they wanted some proof of that.

C: I know. I know.

H: We need a drink.

C: Yeah. We do.

H: Hey, you're gonna move out of this shithole!

Calvin laughs.

C: Yeah.

H: Where you want move to? Up in the hills?

C: Maybe. Maybe downtown.

H: Sure. Lot of nice honeys down there.

C: You know why I moved to the city?

H: Why?

C: Just like you. To see if I could make it. I didn't think it would be like this.

H: What did you think it would be like?

C: Easier.

They laugh together.

H: But did you believe that it was worth it?

C: Sure. You gotta try.

H: And we need to try you now, Calvin.

C: Hobbes.

H: We need to try you now, find out where you might break, where you need shoring up, whether you can lead. Can you lead, brother?

C: What do you mean?

H: Would you be a leader of men?

C: Sure.

H: Ha hya chouhada. From the now into the ever-extended now, our war knows no end, it is all wars. Your hands can help, your eyes, your balls, even. I know that you have balls! How many men can look destiny in the face and not flinch?

C: I don't know.

H: It's a lot to take in. I know.

C: I need a drink.

H: Here.

He hands him his flask. Calvin drinks, drinks again, hands it back.

C: Ah! Thanks.

H: That's what friends are for.

C: Friends.

H: Ready for the revolution.

C: Yeah.

H: And the executions.

C: Yeah.

H: We're gonna write our constitution.

C: I know.

H: There is no restitution.

C: No.

H: For their crimes.

C: No.

H: For their crimes are deep and many. And we have to make them pay.

C: I know. How do we do it.

H: We start with ourselves, Calvin. That's what strong men do. That's what we do, we start with ourselves, we start there and we make sure that we have what it takes, that the weakness we want to eliminate in others has no home in our own bodies, our own habits, our own souls!

C: Wow.

H: It's heavy. (*Hobbes drinks from the flask.*) That's enough of that for now. Calvin, you're like my brother, man, you know that? You're like my brother I never had. Like my brother I never had.

C: You had a brother?

H: Yeah. Yeah I did.

C: What happened to him?

H: He died.

C: I'm sorry.

H: He was a good kid. Just a little stupid, like you. A stubborn motherfucker.

C: How did he die, Hobbes?

H: A training accident. Just an accident.

C: I'm sorry.

H: Yeah. I was sorry too. So we're gonna get you that place up in the hills, huh? Hollywood?

C: Laughs. Yeah. Sure.

H: Come on, aren't you excited?

C: Yeah, you know I am.

H: Because where would I be without you.

C: Yeah.

H: No seriously, where would I be without you? I'd be fucked. I might like to say, I mean I might like to say, sure, I've got pull, I've got connections, but if I'd come back, if I'd come back without you, if I couldn't even bring you along — my oldest friend? — I would have been fucked! Totally fucked. You know that, don't you?

Calvin says nothing.

H: Don't you know what I mean?

C: No. No, I don't.

H: What do you mean, Calvin?

C: I mean I don't know what you mean. I assume they would have killed you.

H: Damn right they would have! Jesus, Calvin! You really do have balls of steel. Just, go easy when it's your time to command. A commander who loves his men, that's, that's a real hero, is who that is.

C: I'm no commander.

H: Yes you are. Yes you are Calvin. You're like a god to me. That's what you are. That's what are you? You believe in Euhemerism?

C: What?

H: That the gods were once men. You believe that?

C: I'm a Catholic.

H: So? You believe you have what it takes to be like God?

C: Sure, like God. But not God himself. You're not God, either, Hobbes. You're a just a man who signed a contract. A man who signed a shitty fucking contract.

H: I believed in it! I believe in it goddamn it! And you better believe in it too! You better! You have to, man!

C: Let's go, huh? Let's get this show on the road.

H: What about the woman?

C: Shit. Juliette.

Calvin goes to the door and looks inside. Hobbes takes out his phone and dials.

H: (*into phone*) Turn it on. He's standing by the closet.

We hear a sound, radiation, from far away. Calvin jerks for a second, stiffens, then he steps into the closet, and closes the door behind him.

Hobbes sits on the bed. He takes a drink from his flask. We see, inside the closet, Calvin sitting calmly. The woman is bound up next to him. He sits and breathes, calmly, his mind far away, far gone.

H: Give me the watchword primeval.
Hold me against the night.
I am a man.
I show you the sign of democracy.
I will have it through you,
My knife, my thought, my life, my love.

I am a man.

He drinks.

I walk, I walk out of the city and into our nation.
I breathe red earth and stone,
I know my kingdom lives in your mind,
And in your heart.

I would have no more families!
I would have no more heartache.

He picks up the phone again and dials.

H: (*into phone*) You can turn it off.

Calvin screams in the closet. He steps out of it.

H: Albemuth liked you.

Spirit Journey

Two men stand in a room.

INTERLOPER: I can see them coming.

THE LISTENER: Where?

INTERLOPER: Into the room.

Lights out. Then lights up on.

—

Two men and a woman sit in a corporate office. They look out the window together on a view of the city.

MAN ONE: It's beautiful.

WOMAN: You can see it, can't you?

MAN TWO: Yeah.

MAN ONE: But what about the government observer?

WOMAN: He'll be fine.

MAN TWO: You mean he's on our side?

WOMAN: I mean he thinks he's on my side.

MAN ONE laughs.

MAN TWO: What are we gonna do with all that money?

MAN ONE: Whatever we want.

Lights out. Then lights up on.

—

INTERLOPER kneels over an intricate pattern of objects he's arranged on the floor, like a mandala.

INTERLOPER: (*whispering*) Almost.

LISTENER: Shall I start?

INTERLOPER: Yeah.

LISTENER: Always when I thought I would depart. Always when I felt their evil in me, their evil pattern in me, my enemy in me, I would doubt my objective, I would lose faith, I would lose control, I would lose heart. Every time I doubted I grew wise, I waited, I waited, for them to come into my hand. Come into my arms, and I will show you something different, from your mast cast against the sky, and your pinot swirling under your nose, I will show you the bouquet of ribboned wreaths acrowding, their eager hearts burning, for your blood . . .

INTERLOPER: Yeah.

INTERLOPER continues to make small adjustments to the objects.

LISTENER: Always before I thought I had gone mad, I thought that there could be nothing that could justify the kind of attention I was giving to these things, these mad things. This mad arrangement of things, myself among them, terrible and mad, my destiny a kind of truth that the world finds unpalatable . . . But always before I knew that someday. Well, that's not true. I had no idea magic was possible.

INTERLOPER: (*looking up at him*) Me neither.

LISTENER: I had no idea the logic of my ancestors was a true logic, truer than many truths I was taught in school. Truer than I ever would have thought . . . until I saw what could happen.

INTERLOPER: If people need it enough.

LISTENER: If people want it enough.

INTERLOPER begins to paint his face.

LISTENER: When do people want it enough?

LISTENER walks around the "mandala", admiring.

LISTENER: When are people willing to listen hard enough?

INTERLOPER: That's your name. Listener.

LISTENER: I know. And you're the interloper.

INTERLOPER: (*laughs*). Yeah, I am. How do I look?

LISTENER: You look good! Are you ready?

INTERLOPER: Yeah.

They both sit near the mandala. They bow their heads and close their eyes.

Lights out. And lights up on

—

MAN TWO: What will we be?

WOMAN: We'll be so beautiful.

MAN ONE: We'll be kings. And you'll be a queen.

WOMAN smiles.

MAN TWO: We thought of it first.

WOMAN: Actually I thought of it first.

MAN ONE: It was a great idea.

MAN TWO: Finders keepers.

Lights out. And lights up on

—

INTERLOPER: Please. Spirits of the universe. Travelers. Take heed to my message. These three people are too greedy; their love too bitter. We would change them if we could but they are too old. Please, spirits, take them with you. Teach them because we can't do it.

LISTENER: Come on spirits.

INTERLOPER: Come on, you beautiful babies.

LISTENER: Have mercy on us.

INTERLOPER: Fuck those motherfuckers up.

LISTENER: We call on you.

INTERLOPER: Fuck those fucking motherfuckers up.

LISTENER: Have mercy on us.

INTERLOPER: Take them away.

LISTENER: Fuck those motherfuckers up.

INTERLOPER: Take them away.

LISTENER: Take them away.

INTERLOPER: Take them away from us.

LISTENER: Liberate us from their philosophy

INTERLOPER: From their enmity

LISTENER: From their logic.

INTERLOPER: From their greed.

LISTENER: Take them!

INTERLOPER sweeps his hand through the "mandala."

Lights out. And lights up on.

—

Blood everywhere. The three corporates are murdered.

Dubya: Operetta

Dubya: Morning, morning, morning.
The sun's comin' up.
My beautiful little Oval.
My beautiful little park.
Condy, I love you.
Laura, I love you.
The sun's comin' up.

Colin. I love you.
I love you, Colin.
Your heart is a mystery to me, I love you.
Colin, Colin!

Colin: Good morning, Mr. President!

Dubya: How's tricks?

Colin: My tricks are good, Mr. President.

Dubya: Colin.

Colin: Mr. President?

Dubya: Colin!

Colin: Yes, Mr. President?

Dubya: Your buttocks are well formed, Colin. They speak to me of distant horizons. Loves lost and unformed. I dreamt of you last night, Colin. I wanted to touch you.

Colin: The UN, Mr. President. The UN.

Dubya: What about those fuckers?

Colin: I'm going, Mr. President. I'm going to convince them. I won't let you down. I won't ever let you down.

Dubya: You're a good boy, Colin. You always were a good boy.

Colin: Don't call me a boy, Mr. President.

Dubya rolls his hand over Colin's head.

Colin: Don't touch my head, Mr. President.

Dubya: It's lucky!

Colin: Yes, Mr. President.

Dubya: Is Condy here?

Colin leaves as Condy enters.

Condy: Yes, Mr. President?

Dubya: Did you see Colin going out? He leaves me. He leaves me. I see him go. I see him go to the UN. I see their smiles, Condy. I see their smiles. I see my father, Condy. Condy. So beautiful, Condy.

Condy: The country loves you, Mr. President. Your mandate is strong. We are strong. We love you. We love you. We love you. We love you, forever and forever into the long beyond.

Dubya: I know you do, Condy. How is the UN doing?

Condy: We have a handle on it, Mr. President.

Dubya: What's Colin saying?

Colin: (*to the UN, unseen*) Thank you, Mr. President. I would like to begin by expressing my thanks for the special effort that each of you made to be here today. 9-11. 9-11. 9-11! Last November 8, this council passed Resolution 1441. Listen: The United States knows about Iraq's weapons of mass destruction.

Dubya: WMD!

Colin: The material I will present to you comes from a variety of sources.Intercepted phone calls, falling from the wire, from the air.Falling, falling, falling, falling.

Dubya: WMD!

Chorus: WMD!

Colin: Saddam is the long dagger in the night. I feel his point. Point for us, my brothers, point for us into his heart. Deny his heart. Deny his heart, that is our. Deny his heart. I remember my father touching my head. Like my President. Like my father. Like my white father. Like my black mother. Like my dying sister. Like my mother, Kofi. Kofi, I see your strong eyes here with us, watching us. Love us and we love you. Love us and we love you.
I'm going down . . .

Chorus: He's going down!

Colin: I'm going down . . .

Dubya: I can feel your heart, Colin. I can feel it beating next to mine.

Colin: I watch you, Mr. President. I watch you so long. I know your face so long. Like a dream. Like a dream I had as a boy, the yellow orb that talked, the smiling yellow dream. You are the orb of my heart, my yellow heart, my fair face formed for you for now, forever.

Dubya: You stand well, Colin. Stand by him. Listen to this one: Once I had a baby,
I put it in the road.
And laughed when heard a crunchy,
From where some tires goed.

Colin: That's awful, Mr. President.

Dubya: Listen to this one:
One fine day in the middle of the night, two dead niggers got up to fight. Back to back they faced each other, drew their swords and shot each other. A dead policeman heard

the noise, and came and killed those two dead nigs.

Colin: I've waited so long to be free.

Dubya: I gaze at your sweet ass in the afternoons. Buttery. Blissful. Unrecorded phantom of desire!

Colin: You're a no one. Mr. President. I'm no one too. I hear your heart beat, black, like me, black, and blacker, and blacker!

Dubya: Touch me . . .

Chorus: Touch him!

Dubya: Touch me!

Chorus: Touch him, Colin! Touch him!

Dubya: The long swathe of your arm is like music. The faint breathe of your silken mouth is like music. Sing to me.

Colin clears his throat, elaborately.

Colin: I am an aspect of your heart's dream, George. George.

Chorus: Geeeeeeeeeeorgie . . . . .

Colin: I loved the Training Corps like I loved my father. Like I love you. The dark blue is so lovely. So lovely. High dress, like high table, the majesty of the poise and the maleness, that maleness like a thick guttered wine in the street, full of sweat and holy music, embittered and hard,

hard to me.

Chorus: Haaaaaaaaaaaard on!   Haaaaaaaaaaaard up! Haaaaaaaard time! Hard time!

Colin: My people. My people.

Dubya: Jungle fever!

Chorus: Jungle Fever!

Colin: Stop that! I was singing!   The Pershing Rifles. The Pershing Rifles! Pershing had the best moustache in town. Better than Hitler's! A good German. A good German, Pershing. Am I a better man now than I once was? Am I a better lover now than I once was? Where will I go now? The UN, the UN, the UN, the red, the red, the reds, the reds!

Dubya: We killed the Reds, come on now Colin.   Come over here.

Chorus: Red!

Colin: Not now

Chorus: Red!

Dubya: Now, Colin.

Colin: I said not now!

Dubya: Now Colin!

Colin: I said not now!

Dubya: Now Colin!

Colin: (*at full volume*) I've lost it all! All my sacred honor! Let me die with the spear through my chest. The spear through my chest like a terrible cock of life and death. Spear me! Spear me! Kill me!

Dubya: I'm sorry, Colin. I didn't know you felt this way.

Colin: It's not your fault. I was a foreigner. A foreigner in my own mind. I came here, to my head, only recently. I'm new in Colin-Town-Head?

Dubya: What the fuck are you talking about?

Chorus: He's mad! Mad mad mad!

Colin: I don't know who . . .

Chorus: (*interrupting*) Mad mad mad mad mad mad!

Colin: (*crying*) I will go into the West. I will diminish. Instead of a dark lord, you will have a queen, beautiful and powerful as the dawn. All shall love me and despair!

Dubya: That's my line. Let's get it the fuck over with already.

They fuck.

Dubya: Oh!

Chorus: Oh!

Colin: Ah! Yes! Harder!

Dubya: Goddamn it!

Colin: Oh!

Chorus: Ahhhhhhhhhhhhhhhhhhhhhh.

Condy comes back.

Condy: Mr. President.

Dubya: We're busy with jungle fever, Condy.

Condy: Mr. President, Obama is here.

Colin becomes Obama.

Dubya: You don't exist. You're only a sort of thing in my dream.

Obama: I'm here for change.

Chorus: Thank God!

Obama: George, where do you keep the cocaine?

Dubya: Umm, over here. I don't touch the stuff, though. Just like to keep it nearby.

Obama: Let's do a line.

Condy, Dubya, and Obama all do lines together.

Dubya: Yummy.

Obama: Double yummy.

Condy: I'm getting wet.

Dubya: We're not interested in that, Condy.

Obama: I must address the people. (*clears throat*). My people. My people. My people.

Chorus: Ahhhhhhhhhhhhhhhhhhhh.

Obama: My people. I have come to you across a long journey. A hard road. I come to you seeking forgiveness, and giving forgiveness. I want to heal our wounds, I want to kiss your babies, I want to give us the chance to succeed.

Chorus: Ahhhhhhhhhhhhhhh.

Obama: We need you. Every last one of you strong, hard working Americans. We are building a dream together. A dream to last a lifetime.

Dubya: My dream!

Chorus: They're so beautiful together!

Dubya: Barack. Tell me you won't, oh tell me you won't, tell me you will not, not now, not ever, tell me who I am.

Obama: Low on the lengths of lawns, the spirit is timed to your awakening. You have coiled the hose. You have lain out your spirits. Love me, here. Love me, here, suburban beauty, love me here in your heart.

Obama transforms back into Colin.

Dubya: Colin, what happened? You were someone else.

Colin: Some civil rights attorney.

Dubya: That was scary. Hold me, Colin.

Colin: Here, Mr. President.

Chorus: Awwwww.

Dubya: Laura loves me, Colin.

Colin: I know, Mr. President.

Dubya: But I love you too.

Condy: Dubois spoke to me last night.

Dubya: Who?

Condy: W.E.B. Dubois. He spoke to me.

Dubya: What did he say?

Colin undergoes yet another transformation into W.E.B. Dubois, this time shaking as though with palsy. The other characters shrink back, afraid.

W.E.B. DuBois: My name is Dubois. Now is the accepted time, not tomorrow, not some more convenient season. It is today that our best work can be done and not some future day or future year. It is today that we fit ourselves for the greater usefulness of tomorrow. Today is the seed time, now are the hours of work, and tomorrow comes the harvest and the playtime.

Dubya: What does it mean?

Chorus: An Ocean! An Ocean is coming! It's coming at us!

Dubya: What?

Chorus: An ocean! An ocean is coming at us!

Dubya: Ayyyyyy! (*shrieks*)

WEB Du bois: The shadow of a mighty Negro past flits through the tale of Ethiopia and of the Egypt the Sphinx. Throughout history, the powers of single blacks flash like falling stars, and die sometimes before the world has rightly gauged their brightness.

Chorus: It's coming. Coming, coming, the wave, the wave, O the Wave!

Dubya: I dreamt of you, wave. I saw your face, like Laura's soft, and sweet, and loving, you came to me and kissed me. You kissed me in the dark, O you black ocean, you loving ocean. Did you see it, Colin?

WEB Du Bois: I am not a violent man. I do not bear arms. But the sight of your face fills me with such dread, that I would fain slaughter you now, than live with your monikers and machinations for the dead days that are coming.

Dubya: You're scary. You're scary! Daddy?

WEB DuBois: I come out of the night. I come here to you. Do you hear me? DO YOU HEAR ME?

There is silence. A solo violin. Then silence. DuBois ducks down and shrinks to the floor. When he arises again, he wipes his brow and is Colin again.

Colin: I need to get some more sleep.

Condy: Pull yourself together, Colin. We're going to take you out of the loop.

Chorus: Out of the loop! Out of sight out of mind! Out of your mind!

Condy: My father taught me respect. He taught me posture. He taught me to smile. Don't I smile well, Mr. President.

Dubya: Sure, honey.

Condy: We need a common enemy to unite us. Without that, we are nothing, I am nothing.

Dubya: Pound those fuckers.

Condy: Transformational Diplomacy is like a cool silk dragon dog, wide and thick, full of awe and shame, the Pale-Faced Fool who watches me while I sleep, counting my veins, waiting for me to wake.

Dubya: You're really great, Condy.

Chorus: You're so great, Condy! (*like tony the tiger*) You're greeeeeeeeat!

Condy: Don't love me. Don't love me. Please. Do not. Do not. Oh, do not. Not now, not ever, I will not in this life feel those ebbing dreams of my other self, my other memory, that first slipping between my legs into a mind's eye that I cannot see, do not show me, O do not show me there, hide me, O hide me.

Dubya: It's OK. Condy. You're taken care of.

Chorus: You're taken care of.

Dubya: Condy, you're good at this shit. I want you to go out. Go out Now.Go Out Now, my black daughter. My beautiful black daughter. Go out Now, and Kill. Kill now, daughter. Look them in the eye and kill. Smile to kill, Laugh to kill. Kill them all, Condy, Kill them all. Every last fucking one of those motherfuckers.

Chorus: Who, Mr. President?

Condy: Yes, who, Mr. President.

Dubya: I saw it in the dream. I remember now. Get this fucking daily brief out of my face, I cant concentrate. Where was I? Oh yes: my dream. The wave was coming at me. The Katrina wave.

Colin: Who, Mr. President?

Dubya: The wave was named Katrina, so beautiful. So beautiful. Awash in the rain, their naked bodies like the Greek Kouros, only dark stone, Gneiss and shale, a Negro wave, with Laura's face, fast, faster, faster! I cut into it with my chisel, my chisel of harmony, my fist, into the rock, into Laura's face. I cut my Laura! My Laura!

Chorus: Ahhhhhhhhhhhhhhhhh.   Ohhhhhhhhhhh.

Dubya: I felt them die. It felt like sex. Like coming. I was coming, and the wave was hitting me. So beautiful.

Condy: Love me. Love me, daddy.

Dubya: Their faces spoke to me. All their colored faces, all colors, in the dark, in the wave, Hell itself, this dream, they spoke to me, lined up and down, their cheekbones shoving from the cool spoke of the curved water, bearing down . . .I am going to be the Memory. It will sink down in Baghdad, into the groundwater. My name. My name is Ozymandias, king of kings, sultan of sultans, lord of the sand and shale and bituminous rock.I hold it, in my hand, dripping black into the sand, and dreaming I sink my hand down into the sands of Baghdad, deep into the groundwater. My hand is a drill. My fingers are corrupted algae, thick algae, buried in the earth, migrating, migrating downwards. Downwards to the Dolostone.

Chorus: Dolostone. Dolostone! What's dolostone?

Dubya: Oil! Oil! Oil of my heart. Anoint my head with oil. Free me, free me, Condy, Colin, O free me! Free me!

Condy: But who should we kill?

Dubya: I saw their faces in the wave, there in the sand. In the dolostone. In the rock, in the desert. I will drive my hand down. Down into the rock. Kill them all, Condy. God help me do it.Let him guide my hand down into the rock, the Plymouth Rock, theMighty Rock, the lodestone rock, the Gibraltar of my inner eye,there in the dark Baghdad night.

Condy: But who should we kill?

Dubya: My father loved them. I love them. Kill them, Condy. Kill them all.

Condy: Yes, Mr. President.

Colin: Yes, Mr. President.

Chorus: Yes, Mr. President.

The Jump

Lights up on a man standing alone in dim light, wearing a suit without a tie.

MAN: We're going, honey. You and I, we're going. Don't be afraid. Just hold on. I've taken care of everything. The children are in the back, asleep, they're dreaming.
What do you think? Do you believe me now? You said it would never happen but it is, it's happening. My love. The stars are so bright, but they're growing dimmer, and other stars, you see them? Honey, do you see them, they're coming out! Like it was just for us. Hold my hand.

He smiles and laughs a little, with soft amazement.

MAN: All these years, Alice — no, don't think about it. . . . stacked up like cordwood, like in Auschwitz. Hold my hand.There, the engines. Oh, it's like a dream, Alice. I know, I know. We'll find out, what can I say? We'll find out when we get there.The law's delay and the insolence of office. But there are no more offices now, are there? No more prison cells. They never put you in one. But I heard your voice in mine.

Do you feel like you're sleeping. How funny. Like dying, like we're slipping out of this old life, this old sun, this old whirling world and someone just gave us a magnet, a big terrific magnet and said "here you go, try this" . . . and then you'll get away, oh, you'll get away, you'll get away, you'll get away . . .

Suddenly he is distraught, peering about the stage, looking for his dead friends.

MAN: Mercury? Einstein? I have to wash my hands, I'm sorry! Mercury, where did you go?

Slowly he recovers.

MAN: Oh, no, no. We're here. I don't think it'll take long, honey. They didn't say it would take long. (*Singing*) The stars are wide and alive . . . (*softer, speaking*) . . . but will not ever tell me who I am. Yes, the children are asleep, don't worry. We were in adjacent cells, you see, Mercury, Einstein and me. And after the blast, I was alone.

MAN: You remember when you said "it'll be better after the coronation," you were making a salad, it was November, a week before Thanksgiving, our son was two. And I quoted the goddamned Little Green Book and said, "whatever their offense, no one shall receive no more than one hundred blows." No one shall receive more than one hundred blows. No one shall receive more than one hundred blows. No one shall receive more than one hundred blows . . .

Shhhh, it helps me to talk. I'm scared too. We'll be OK. It's just like getting on a plane. You get on, and the flight attendant smiles at you, okay, we don't have a flight attendant, I'll be the flight attendant, okay? Chivas and soda for you, darling? Would you care for some peanuts? Little pretzels shaped like Christmas trees?

. . . But it was like coming back from the dead. And you think you're dead too.

What, stop it! Stop it! Stop it! Stop crying.

The lights have grown strange.

MAN: Shhhh, there's others here. Don't say anything.

There are strange sounds and lights.

MAN: Just hold my hand. Other travelers is all, honey. The children are asleep, you go to sleep too, if you want, I'll be here. (*Pause*) They smell like cardamom, these people. Cinnamon and cardamom. Shhhhh, shhhh, shhhh. Go to sleep. Just other people like us, passing through the dark.

What is it they say? A place for all the things we don't have words for here. Maybe they'll even get rid of pain. No, got to keep pain. Maybe they'll get rid of happiness. I could live with that. As long as I have you, Alice. My secret happiness with you, that's what I'll have. No matter what happens.

We passed by them. (*Pause*) Interstitial. In between the stitches of the world. You'll sew when we get there, Alice, you will. You can make a new dress! A new yellow dress. A summer dress, for a summer world. Oh, don't cry. Don't cry.

Blackout. Lights up, red, shifting lights.

MAN: It's not my blood! It's not my blood!

He laughs hysterically, then quiets.

MAN: Not my blood. I collaborated. Yes, with the invaders! Hahahaha! They were smarter than you, assholes! Einstein? Einstein!

Lights return to normal. We hear wind.

MAN: I don't want to write an epitaph. But I can't get the idea out of my head, like some bad Douglas Adams line from Hitchhiker's Guide to the Galaxy, Earth, yes, just "mostly harmless." But you had plenty of harm left to do at the end, didn't you?

Who else do you think goes this way? The Neighbors?

We hear more eerie sounds.

MAN: No, I didn't mean it! Better not to think about them. The stars are all gone now, Alice, I didn't even notice, I was distracted. All gone.

Maybe they knew David Ives, did you ever think of that? Maybe they met him, the playwright, Alice, you know. Maybe they met him in his hometown. And they told him the story of Green Hill. I told you, that was when I knew who to believe, didn't I, Alice? After I saw that beautiful play . . . I mean, for him in that play the Green Hill was like Death, wasn't it? Going towards death, but it's so much else . . .

Because he saw that Green Hill and he knew he had to get there, no matter what. No matter what.

And now we can say whatever we want to, Alice, do whatever we want to, like the Statue of Liberty is just up ahead and just a little delousing, just a little poison and then through to New York . . .

We're going to jump, Oh my God, we're going to jump . . .

Lights up to full, distorted bright white. Then blackout.

Two Jews

Scene 1

A: Jew!

B: Jew!

A: Brother

B: Brother.

A: How are you?

B: I've been better.

A: How are you really?

B: I'm alive. Aren't I?

A: Sure.

B: And how are you?

A: The light felt good this morning.

B: That's nice.

A: Yes.

B: Why did it feel good?

A: Sometimes it does.

B: I'm sinking.

A: Why?

B: I'm not sure.

A: Brother.

B: Brother.

A: Tell me, brother.

B: Yes.

A: Why are you a Jew?

B: It's what I am, brother.

A: Why?

B: You know why.

A: Tell me again. Tell me again.

B: Why? Are you recording me?

A: No, I want to remember. I want to hear it again.

B: I am a Jew. I am a Jew among the Jews. Among the many Jews, I am a Jew. I had my briss, I worship God.

A: You worship God?

B: Yes.

A: How do you do that?

B: You've been to temple, brother.

A: But I never understood it.

B: Neither did I.

A: Why are you a Jew, brother?

B: Why is anyone a Jew and not something else? It's how I was raised, how I was born. I am a man! I am a Jew!

A: Which is first?

B: A man.

A: A man?

B: A Jew.

A: A Jew?

B: I hate you, brother.

A: Could you be a Jew and not be a man?

B: Not be human, you mean?

A: Yes, if you like.

B: Is that what you like?

A: Yes.

Barry stands.

B: Tell me, brother. Why aren't you a Jew?

A: I renounced it.

B: As though we would let you do that.

A: Yes.

B: Tell me why, brother.

A: Why what?

B: Why I am a Jew and you are not.

A: I don't know.

B: You do.

A: No.

B: You do know.

A: I am in a different story. My life is different. We're both Americans.

B: An American Jew.

A: American Jew.

B: I am an American Jew.

A: And I am an American Goy Boy.

B: Well, a goyim anyway. But not really. You're still a Jew.

A: I can never leave.

B: Not with your blood, you can't.

A: So it's in the blood.

B: You know it is.

A: So I can never leave.

B: The Nazis would still kill you, wouldn't they? German, American, or whatever.

A: I will dance.

B: I will kill.

A: I will screech at the moon.

B: I will howl like a cat.

A: I will ape my betters. I will grow, and make a maze. I will build a city in the desert.

B: Like Moses.

A: Moses didn't build any cities, come on now.

B: Let us dance together.

The brothers dance, to the cello, the cellist, who comes out. They dance a dance of the shtetl.

A: I am weeping brother.

B: We are only men.

A: But Jews first.

Barry screams. Abel keeps dancing.

B: I am a biped in the desert. I am a Canaanite.

Cellist: Let us speak of the Canaanites.

A: In the land of Canaan.

B: What a bad idea.

A: But it could have been any place.

B: But it was that one. An accident of geography and tectonic plates. Is your mother an accident? Am I an accident, brother? Were the Germans an accident?

A: You're part German.

B: Just like you.

A: Why are we on about this anyway?

B: Something has happened.

A: Happened? What's happened?

B: We're in power, brother.

A: What?

B: We rule the city.

A: What city?

B: This one.

A: When did this happen?

B: Last night.

A: What?

B: Last night we decided.

A: Decided to be more active.

B: Yes. Decided to do our duty to our ancestors.

A: To the Canaanites.

B: To the Jewish People, brother.

A: But which ones?

B: Storyteller.

A: Which ones?

B: All of us, brother.

A: All of us.

B: All us Jews.

A: If only.

B: It's more or less true.

A: Some conspiracy theory.

B: If you like.

A: I don't want any part of it.

B: What will you do, brother?

A: I'll fight you.

B: Why? You would betray us?

A: Tell me, Barry. It was just a bad dream you had, hmm? Your wife, she's been ill. Your son, he doesn't call. That was it, hmm? Let's have a drink.

B: I will tell you what it is. Our walls are crumbling. A pogrom can always come. It can always come. It can always come.

A: And why did they come brother?

B: A judgment of God.

A: Nonsense.

B: We are always hated.

A: Why is that, brother?

B: Even when we assimilate. Even when we serve their kings and charm their daughters. Even when we convert to their religions, we are hated. We are always, always hated! This is why we keep watch. Why we remember. You know all this, asshole.

A: What a powerful story, eh?

B: More than a story.

A: Like the Christians.

B: What did you say?

A: There are enemies all about! Amalek is everywhere! Around every turn! Men! There are men! There are men with swords! There are men with swords! They have different eyes!

Barry says nothing.

A: Amalek! Amalek must be stamped out! Amalek! Down with Amalek! Down with the world beneath the world! Down with Muir and his Barkonauts!

B: Have you been taking drugs?

A: I am a Jew.

B: So you admit it.

A: I am ashamed.

Barry laughs.

B: I love you, brother.

A: I am ashamed of you, of us.

B: So am I, brother. But you cannot let that paralyze you. Where would be without our shame? Inhuman. It makes us men.

A: Give me a drink.

Barry pours him a drink and he drinks.

B: How is your business?

A: My business is fine. And yours?

B: Oh, can't complain.

They sit, and drink.

A: So, there was a decision.

B: Hard to believe, I know.

A: Yes, Jews agreeing on something?

Barry laughs.

B: And yet we did. We agreed we must be more vigilant. That times are growing more dangerous.

A: And what would Moses do?

B: To hell with Moses. What are we going to do, eh? What are you going to do?

A: You're really talking about a Jewish Conspiracy.

B: I know, kind of sexy, isn't it?

A: Not a conspiracy, I suppose. Articles of Confederation, perhaps?

B: Oh, we didn't write anything down.

A: No.

B: Do you trust me, brother?

A: Sometimes.

B: That's all?

A: That's all.

B: That's disappointing.

A: Sorry to disappoint you.

B: What will you do, brother?

A: What will you do, Barry? With these articles of confederation?

B: You're a lunatic.

A: Yes, perhaps.

B: I am a lunatic, too.

A: Let us be lunatics together.

B: Our calendar is lunar, after all.

A: Whatever that means.

B: What will we do? We rule. We are kings. God help us.

Abel says nothing.

B: We are judges of men. We are princes of our cities. Our daughters princesses. We are known the world over for our wisdom and our wealth, and our learning. We abide and we keep and we grow and we keep our silences and our mysteries, we dance as our ancestors did, we keep our faith and covenants, we are diplomats and sailors and soldiers, and we are in charge, brother. We are in charge.

A: Pretty words.

B: But this is our problem. We need more Jews. We are vulnerable.

A: More Jews?

B: We are too few. A pogrom may come. Another Shoah, to sweep us from the table of the earth like chaff.

A: God forbid.

B: God may not forbid it.

A: So, Jewish prince, how may I advise thee?

B: I would make my kingdom strong.

A: It is strong, prince. Amalek is far away.

B: And close too.

A: Well, you're supposed to keep them close, aren't you?

B: Like a brother.

A: You are my brother!

B: Yes.

A: Brothers by a different mother!

B: And so it is.

A: I hate you for that.

B: And so you should. Your mother was a whore.

They fight. After a while, they tire.

A: You're an asshole.

Barry pants.

B: It will be good for your business if you help. Good for your daughter.

A: My daughter is fine.

B: What is it that you want?

A: Same as you.

B: But not the same.

A: Same enough.

B: Mmm.

A: I don't care that you're a Jew. But I care that you're a prince. Jews are better out of power than in. We keep the princes honest. As princes we are greedy men.

B: No.

A: Oh, yes. Like Solomon. With his hundred wives, or two hundred.

B: It was the fashion of the times.

A: He was show off. Like you.

B: What would you have, Abel? You would have us be beggars again? Tinkers on the road?

A: Are there any Jewish tinkers left?

B: Somewhere, I'm sure.

A: You have none of the wisdom of a tinker.

B: Yes I do.

A: Perhaps you do.

B: I do.

A: What is the wisdom of the tinker, brother?

B: To watch the road, and the sky above the road. To repair your shoes. To find, to find and give away, and trade. To trade a mop for a tin for a pan for a tooth. To sing quiet, by the fire. To sing like the Canaanites under the stars, unknown, by a woman, by your son, to sing of the message your father gave to you, and his father, and his father before him, and his father before him, and his father before him, and his father before him, etc, etc, etc, etc, etc, etc . . .

A: I move a dream across an ocean! To Jerusalem!

There is a sigh.

B: I count the fish that I will catch! I tell you, I tell you, American,. I am a Jew! I am a man with only one hat, and two shoes. I am a man who cannot remember the way home!

A: From my mother, from my mother, from my mother. My grandmother. My grandmother and my grandmother. My grandmother. But where are the grandmothers.

B: A Jew comes!

A : There is a Jew here Max!

B: Show me your braunen augen.

A: On the opposite platform.

B: On the U-Bahn.

A: Take me to Jerusalem Max!

B: No.

A: Take me to the city of our ancestors!

B: You must go yourself.

A: I will kill a thousand times! I will die! I will die in Jerusalem!

B: You're hallucinating.

A: I am Amalek. Abel Amalek. I am your brother. I will cut off your cock with a stone. I will mark your face with my knife. You will scream the name of my gods.

B: Rather lurid, isn't it?

A: Brother.

B: Brother.

A: What will you do, now?

B: It's only a charity. A Jewish charity.

A: For the poor Jews.

B: There are still poor Jews.

A: What does it mean, brother? What does this century mean for us?

B: Trade. It means trade.

A: Yes.

B: Lessons.

A: Yes.

B: Murthers!

Abel laughs.

A: Murthers!

Barry smiles.

B: I love you, brother.

A: I love you, too.

B: We must hide from the Poles.

A: And the Russians.

B: And the Czechs.

A: And the Lithuanians.

B: And the Bello-Russians.

A: And the Turks.

B: And the Armenians.

A: And the Syrians.

B: And the Arabs.

A: The Arabs.

B: And the Canadians.

Abel laughs.

A: A pogrom in Canada.

B: That's awful.

A: It's no joke. We must beware the Canadians.

Barry laughs.

A: So you do have some of the wisdom of the tinker.

B: Yes.

A: But a prince cannot be a tinker.

B: No.

A: But you have some of the wisdom of the tinker.

B: Some.

A: Of the ragman.

B: The nomad.

A: The Wandering Jew!

B: We were farmers, goddamn it. Like everyone.

Abel laughs.

A: With our marker stones.

B: Yes.

A: It's just a rock.

B: It's my rock.

A: Say I were to say, perhaps the rock should be by the tree instead?

B: I see you have an opinion!

A: The rabbi says in my great-grandfather's time that's just where the marker was!

B: He is a wise rabbi.

A: And I say it was your great-grandfather moved it! Moved the marker in the night!

Barry laughs.

B: Can't the farmer and the cowman be friends?

A: I will punish the sun. I will punish Ra for our heresies.

B: We used to worship it, you know.

A: What didn't we worship! Omnivores, all of us. Pan, Baal, Astarte. Our sanity extended only as far as our bodies.

B: And sometimes not even that far.

A: A Jew is a Jew. We love Jews!

They dance.

B: A Jew is a Jew!

A: Because a Jew is a Jew!

B: A Jew is not Amalek!

A: Because a Jew is a Jew!

B: Unless an Amalek is a Jew, in which case he's an Amaleki Jew!

A: And therefore a Jew!

B: Of our thirteen tribes!

A: Or Fourteen!

B: And we will rule.

A: And we will live.

B: Beneath the stars.

A: I can see heaven coming!

B: I can feel Jesus coming!

Abel laughs.

A: And Moses!

B: Which one!

Abel laughs.

A: I feel the Earth move. I feel the sky dance!

B: There is something hovering over the water! What is it!

A: A sign from God!

B: Which one!

A: Skyfather!

B: What does Baal want?

A: A sacrifice!

B: A woman!

A: A love!

B: He's lonely.

A: To hell with Baal, we need to get out of here!

B: Hold my hand.

They hold hands.

A: I am a body.

B: I am a body.

A: I am a brother.

B: I am your brother.

A: By a different mother.

B: What of the widows!

A: What of the Jewish widows!

B: They are so young!

A: They are so young.

B: We should make them Jews!

Abel, weeping, lets go of his brother's hand, and skips about the stage.

A: I am totonka!

Abel gets down on all fours as a buffalo. Barry laughs.

B: I am Barry Goldwater!

A: Mooooooo.

B: Abel, you have upset one of my marker stones! I must be compensated!

A: Mooooooo!

B: I must consult the rabbi.

Abel becomes the rabbi.

A: What seems to be the problem, Barry?

B: My totonka, it has upset one of my marker stones.

A: This is grave. A problem for the Jewish people.

B: Yes rabbi.

A: Let me consult the scrolls.

B: Yes rabbi.

A: How is your wife?

B: She is well, thank you, rabbi.

A: A pretty little thing.

B: Yes rabbi. What should I do about my totonka?

A: Let me consult the scrolls.

Abel turns around then turns back around.

A: I have consulted our scrolls.

B: What do they say, rabbi?

A: Many things.

B: Yes, rabbi.

A: About your totanka, I am not sure. Many years ago, in the time of King David, a Jew hit a totanka with his staff, and the totanka changed into a man. And King David went to his brother, his eldest brother, to ask for advice. "God has made my totanka into a man! Our family is cursed!" he said. "We must go to the rabbi," said David's eldest brother. But the rabbi was asleep. And he would not wake up. And the totanka who had become a man urged David and his people to build evil idols in the shape of the totanka, and so those people perished.

B: Rabbi?

A: Your totanka is not just a totanka. It is a sign of the covenant between God and Man. So as we care for our animals, they care for us. If an animal does a wrong to you, you must forgive the animal. It is only an animal. It does what animals do, as we do.

B: But rabbi, the totanka has upset my marker stone.

A: Then put it back, idiot. This is a problem for a rabbi?

Barry sits down. Abel wanders about the stage.

A: What will you do, Jew?

B: Rule.

Blackout.

Scene 2

The Director sits in his chair, directing Actress.

D: Stand in an arbitrary place. Depending on your judgment. Where you judge it, stand.

She picks a place, changes her mind, picks another place, changes her mind, picks a third place and stands there.

D: Judge.

A: Who is here?

D: A woman, and a man.

A: What are their names?

D: Angelika, and Barry.

A: Let them speak.

D: They cannot speak.

A: No?

D: No.

A: How do I judge them?

D: You must judge them in silence.

A: How did I do that?

D: When I was a boy I felt the sun on my face and knew that the burn of the sun was a mark of tradition, was a way for me to escape school, if I was burned enough, if I was burned enough, if I was enough myself, if I ran long enough, if I could only run away.

When I was a boy I knew that I could find a way to be myself, I knew I could find a way to no longer be a Jew, I knew I could find a way to no longer be a man, I knew I could find a way to escape.

Long ago when I was a boy I held the jar in my hand and I was sanctified and I would have none of it any more, I would let it go, I would undo the bonds of my ancestors who won so many battles, I would escape, I would give it all away.

A: When I was a girl I knew I was something special. I knew I would have more, and less, I knew it would hurt, I knew that it was good that it would hurt, I knew that in the long run I would find my man and my valley, and my sons, my many sons!

When I was a little girl I held a boy in my arms and I whispered my name into his ear. And my name was meaningless! When I was a girl I looked in my father's eyes and told him that I wanted to go to Mars! And my father scolded me. And I still want to go.

D: When I was a boy I felt the look of the others. I felt the look of the goyim. I felt the look of the others. I felt the look of my mother. I felt the look of the rabbi. I felt the look of my father. I felt the hand of God, in my dreams, I felt the arm of the universe, bending towards justice, mocking me, caring for me, holding me, remembering me, advising me in this horrifying march, in this horrifying march out of the Jewish ghetto and into the city, back into the city at last, back at last into the city of our people.

A: I am woman.

D: Judge us.

A: I am woman. I have had so many names. I have knelt in so many temples. I have climbed so many trees, with my sisters.

D: And now you are on Earth.

A: I am still in the trees! I have remembered so many scratches of the back! I have counted the nits in your fur and watched the moon, I have watched the moon and crawled into the berth of the branches, I have lain awake at night and wondered, how did I come to be! How did I come to be me, a woman?

D: Judge us. Woman.

A: I have a candle and I have a match. I have a word, only a sound, the syllable is not important, only the tone, like the tone of a symphony, like the tone of my son's voice, ringing forth to war!

D: Judge us!

A: I desire war! I desire war forever! I am the sparkle of your bones! I am Egypt, come from your rest! I am magnificence divine! I am the particles of your gods! The stardust of old! I am gold, mapped into your Jewish hat! I am the Rah, I am the Raja! I am the long night! I am the long and winding night! I am the vulture who will care for you in the mountain! I am the darkness that grew you into a man! I am the long night, the long and winding night, I am the sobbing barber shop that will carry you away!

D: Judge the stars, then, woman, draw us a map.

A: I am the murmur in your sleep! I am the thighs that wrap around your body. I am the long arc of Mars. I am the right arm, I am the Magellanic arm of science, wrought hard and brittle for our brothers, to fight Amalek.

D: Judge Amalek, then, woman!

A: What would it mean? What would it mean to judge them?

D: They are the enemy. They must be judged.

A: Enemies are for killing. Why should we judge them?

D: It is what we do.

A: Why?

D: Stand in an arbitrary place!

She moves, and moves, and stands.

D: Hold your position!

She sings.

D: Hold!

She sings.

D: Hold!

She sings.

D: Hold out your life! Hold them tight! Hold your son before you cast him into the fire!

She sings.

Scene 3

The Cellist plays.

Scene 4

A: I have consulted the scrolls.

B: I have consulted them too.

A: I have wept for my ancestors.

B: I have wept for myself.

A: I have grown old.

B: I have known too much.

A: I still do.

B: If we will rule justly, if we will know wisdom, if we will protect our children and our neighbor's children, if we will feed the widows and the strangers, if we will do that we will stay strong, we will stay Jews.

A: Yes.

B: But I fear that we will not do this. I fear we will lose everything, everything.

A: Yes.

B: What did the scrolls tell you?

A: In the theater of conflict, in the theater of war and peace, our fire is still burning, brother. Our hearth fires burn. Our cholla is baking. Our honey and apples are safe. The hlafweird, the bread-keeper, he keeps our hearth safe, and I am hlafweird, brother, I keep the hearth fire and the bread safe. In the theater of our valley we are listening for a cue, brother, listening for the sound of war and of suspicion, we sharpen our swords and train our men and women, howling into the night like wolves, dancing to keep the devils out, plowing our fields, but I see something now on the horizon, the Jew is coming.

B: The Jew is coming?

A: The Jew is coming, brother.

B: Surely not.

A: I see him with his staff, like Gandalf.

B: That old son of a bitch.

A: The Jew is coming. Our Jew.

B: Not ours, not our Jew.

A: The Jew is ours, he is our Jew. The most stubborn Jew in the shtetl.

B: Damn the Jew. To hell with him.

A: Still, here he is. I am the Jew. I am come to you.

B: Yes.

A: I am leaving the shtetl!

B: But you just got here!

A: Jew.

B: I am a Jew!

A: But what of the Jews who are not Jews.

B: They are Jews too.

A: But they are Jews too.

B: They are Semites.

A: I am leaving the shtetl!

B: But you just got here!

A: I am not going to Babylon!

B: But we're all going!

A: I am not!

B: You should come with us!

A: I will not.

B: You are a Jew. You should come with your people.

A: Jew from Yehuda, the celebrated. The praised. That is who the Jews are, before they were Chosen, they were celebrated! Like elementary school, first you get popular, then you get elected.

B: Yes, yes.

A: We were popular in the Levant!

B: Quite popular!

A: We were celebrated.

B: And still are!

A: Quite naturally. We do well in school.

B: Yes, yes.

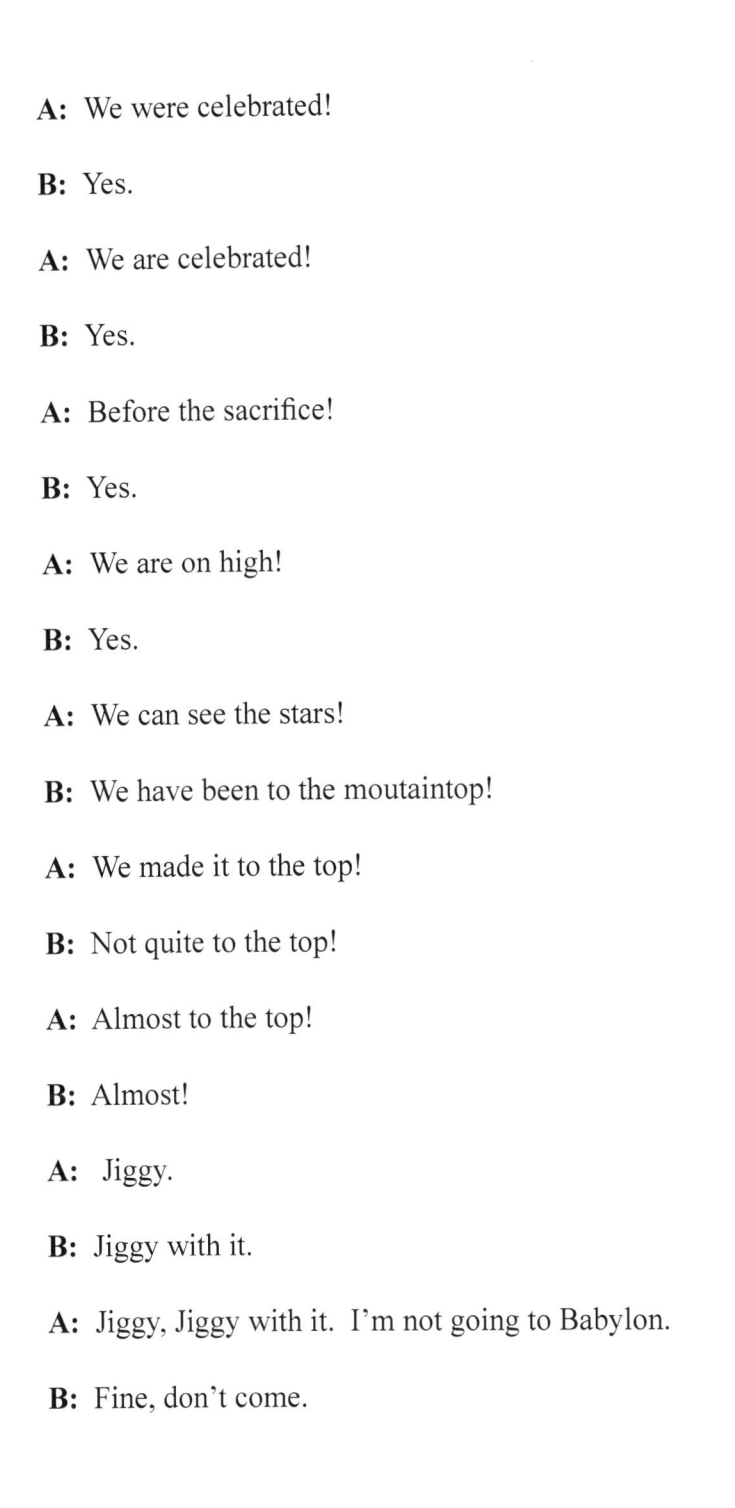

A: We were celebrated!

B: Yes.

A: We are celebrated!

B: Yes.

A: Before the sacrifice!

B: Yes.

A: We are on high!

B: Yes.

A: We can see the stars!

B: We have been to the moutaintop!

A: We made it to the top!

B: Not quite to the top!

A: Almost to the top!

B: Almost!

A: Jiggy.

B: Jiggy with it.

A: Jiggy, Jiggy with it. I'm not going to Babylon.

B: Fine, don't come.

A: I won't.

B: Then you will no longer be a Jew!

A: Fine.

B: No longer celebrated!

A: Fine!

B: Like Ing, I will go East!

A: Go and do it then!

B: I will! We will all go to Babylon and accept our fetters!

A: Nonsense.

B: And we will be re-arranged.

A: Once celebrated, we became the unlucky.

B: Ugly baby!

A: We were winning too much at cards!

B: We only won once!

A: But we never shut up about it!

B: I am the white!

A: I am the red!

B: I am the majesty of Fate!

A: I am the old gold sun of your son, the wand he kept in a box, the herald, the herald wolf!

B: Nonsense you speak.

A: The Jews were the misfortune of Warsaw!

B: Unlucky.

A: But we will win at cards again.

B: In Babylon we will win, we will win ourselves a language.

A: But not I.

B: Come with us, Jew.

A: I am not a Jew.

B: Come with us out of Canann! Come with us like Ing! The man who went East!

A: To Babylon, eh?

B: To the gate of the gods!

A: Never, never.

B: Back into the garden!

A: Never, never.

B: You will be forgotten.

A: Fine with me.

B: We just want to be more awesome. Don't you want to be awesome any more?

A: I don't want to be more awesome.

B: Yes you do.

A: I will stay in the shtetl. Even if alone, I will stay.

B: The Russians will kill you.

A: Perhaps.

B: They will.

A: I have lain my marker stone down by my ox: down by my totanka. I shall not be moved.

B: So you say. I say the marker stone belongs over by the tree.

A: Stay with me.

B: I must go. I need new gods: new women. Come with me.

A: I must stay. My farm is here.

B: There are other farms. We will bring our scrolls.

A: I will keep my scroll here. I will bury it.

B: Why will you do this mad thing?

A: What else can I do, brother? This land is mine. I am part of it. My wife is here, my children.

B: It is the same for me. Come with us. You will be lonely.

A: So will you.

B: My stone will always stand here, even when it is gone.

A: I will always be with you.

B: Hold me.

They embrace.

A: I will tell you a story.

B: Oh my God.

A: Once upon a time, we dwelt here. We were upon the time, and it was upon us. We commingled in our desperation with the blood of the lan**D:** we were upon the time and it was upon us. We could not escape that spirit, the spirit of the land, the spirit of our fathers, binding us down, insisting on our obligations, remembering our so many trespasses past the boundary stones, past the gate of the gods, and other gates, and other gods, all remembered, remembered too long.

B: How will I remember you?

A: Only write me down. Tell your sons, remind them. Write me down.

B: I'll miss you.

A: Don't get sentimental.

B: But you won't go through the gate.

A: No.

B: How will I remember?

A: You will.

B: The memory gate.

A: Yes.

B: I cannot remember past the gate. The words, the letters, they will make me forget.

A: But you will remember too. Somewhere you will. Somewhere you will always be remembered, we will always remember.

B: Like elephants.

A: Yes.

B: Stand at an arbitrary place, arbiter.

A: Yes.

Abel stands, moves, stands firm.

B: Judge us, arbiter.

A: If you can't be just, be arbitrary. Make the decision. Cut the twine, open the package, pass through the gate having bribed the guard, bow down before the idol but whisper another name, marry a woman but call her by the name of your grandmother, only in private. We shall be name**D:** we shall be rearranged.

B: Judge us, arbiter.

A: I am one of the judges. I am come to you. I come and I go, to you. Not of you but next to you, I speak of the precedents, of history, I mark and map, I draw the line in the sand and the scar on your flesh, I determine the boundary.

B: At an arbitrary place.

A: I am one of the judges. My men are wise and faithful, this makes them judges. To be wise, to be faithful. Faith in each other first. Faith that we can work it out.

B: Inspired by God!

A: Inspired by you, brother. And in hate of you. In my judgment I am remove. I am the instinct that knows the crow, I am the crone who knows which stone to throw. I am the ugly baby! Ugly baby!

B: Let Skyfather be appeased!

A: I am the Ugly Baby. I bow, I bow. I cover my head. I shield you. I am the token of our long slide down. I am the scepter of the light. I am the mark of your division. I am the entropy who binds you to this Earth.

B: You confuse me, brother.

A: I know so many names. I know so many. What is yours?

B: You know me, brother. I am Barry.

A: And my name is Abel. You are Barry, from Finnabarr, the Spear. You are Spear. And I am Abel, the Breath, the son, the breathing spirit, the inspiration.

B: I am an Irish Spear.

A: I am a Breathing Spirit.

B: Stand at an arbitrary place.

A: I stand here.

B: What is your judgment.

A: The same. You will go. You will settle. You will be poor. You will be rich. You will be poor. You will know many women. You will be cast out.

B: That is a prophecy. What is your judgment?

A: To set, and put. To condemn. To doom us together. To doom us in our maps. To draw the right passageways with chalk.

B: What do you set on me? Where do you put me? What is my doom?

A: As I said. You will go. You will seek. I put you where you are.

B: Let's have a drink.

They pour, and drink.

A: It is exhausting, being Jews.

Barry says nothing.

A: They say we knew 9-11 was coming.

B: They want a pogrom.

A: They let us in.

B: So did the Germans.

A: When will it end?

B: When we are dead.

A: When will it end for us?

B: That is why we made the agreement.

A: Why did you?

B: We must prepare.

A: Prepare for what?

B: For war, for war.

A: God help us.

B: God may not.

A: Let's have a drink.

B: I've had enough. I should go.

A: Already?

B: My wife will be worried.

A: Call her then.

Barry takes out his cel phone and dials. Abel finishes his drink.

B: Honey? Are you OK? He did what? Ridiculous. I'll be home soon. I don't know what to tell him. Tell him whatever you want. I'll be home soon. No, I don't know. Okay. Bye.

He hangs up.

B: Why not come over? Have dinner with us.

A: Okay.

B: Bring some of that wine you like.

A: The Pinot?

B: The Pinot.

They walk, in the light. They dine, with Barry's wife, Charlotte.

C: So the rabbi says to me, did you make the cholla? And I say, yes, Rachel, I did, would you like some? "Your cholla?" She says. "I have a cold."

A: She is such a weird rabbi.

C: She's sweet though.

Barry pours wine for all and toasts.

B: To the Obama years!

C: To our new charity!

A: And to you, brother.

B: The farmer and the cowman can be friends.

Charlotte laughs.

C: I am a woman.

A: There's no mistaking that.

C: I came down from the trees.

The men watch her expectantly.

C: I received a signal.

B: Not yet.

C: I received a signal, and I came down.

B: Not yet.

C: I received a signal and I came down from the trees. In my hips, in my walk, in my posture, in my memory, in my heart.

They watch her.

A: They're delicious hips.

C: And you men grew smaller, and we grew larger. Almost the same size. Almost the same size. Sometimes we're even bigger than you. And you went away. You went away. You went away, men. You ran away.

B: We had to.

C: Why?

B: To live.

A: This is depressing. Anyone seen any good movies or anything?

C: I don't go to the movies any more.

A: Why not?

C: Too depressing. All that propaganda.

A: Just good clean American entertainment.

C: I don't know how clean it is. What will we do, gents?

B: About?

A: What do you want to do, Charlotte?

C: Change the world.

A: Don't we all.

B: What will you do, woman?

C: Something.

A: What?

She stands.

C: I came out of the trees.

A: Well, not you personally.

B: What will you do?

C: Dance.

She dances, very very slow. Barry claps with her, slow. Abel sings

A: I am a Jew within the land.
I am a Jew with a broken heart.
I will never have a home.
We threw all our homes away.
For a home unassailable,
Within.

Her dance becomes angrier.

A: I sing of pain,
A pain we won't forget.
I sing of the kingdom,
I sing of the kingdom,
I sing of our Jewish dominions.
I sing of the long light,
And the long sun,
I sing of the high king,
And the higher prize,
Illustrious,
Unnameable.

B: I sing of the tree,
The Jewish Tree,
Spinning in the dark,
The light that darkens eyes,
That darkens Jewish souls,
I sing of the wail at noon,
And the spine,
The backbone divine,
The mercury of wine,
The tale we can't untell.

She dances faster. Abel speaks.

A: Out from a dark city, under the aegis of our thoughts, you and I brother, and this woman, we will uncover all our pains from old. We will remember tinker's things! We will remember the pain of the Jew!

She dances even more angrily. And she sings.

C: When will I be delivered?

What message can I deliver?
Can not a woman be the Messiah?
To end the awful waiting?
We're already now,
Already now between,
We have it upon us,
This mess of life,
This sway of land,
My sagging breasts,
My children,
Far and gone.
When will I be named?
When will I be allowed to forget?

The men leave. She lies down to go to sleep.

A boy comes out onto stage and sits in a chair.

BOY: I can endure. I can endure anything. I am a prince. I am a prince at sea. I am at sea. I wind through the waves. I am an adventurer! I will go on! I will go on! I will go on and on!

Abel comes out.

A: Son, you will go on, but you will not forget.

BOY: No, I will not forget.

A: You will remember.

BOY: Yes, I will remember.

A: You will remember my name.

BOY: Yes, father.

A: And yours.

BOY: Yes.

A: Never forget that. What will you tell them, son, over the sea?

BOY: That I'm strong.

A: Yes. Never tell them you're a Jew.

BOY: What am I?

A: My son. You're my son.

BOY: What else should I tell them?

A: Nothing else, son. You tell them whatever they need to hear.

A Man Stands

An empty space. A Man stands, one foot in front of the other, balancing. A Iago-type whisperer comes next to the Man, and hunches next to his ear, stage-whispering loudly.

IAGO: Cement your bond. Balance. See the horizon. You are on the horizon. Focus on the horizon and you are part of it.

The Man bends his head downward slightly.

IAGO: Humility is a virtue. Be penitent. But not too penitent. See how your head hangs slightly? You submit before a higher authority: God, your neighbors, your elders. You are in equipoise but you have lost the horizon. Look up.

He looks up again.

IAGO: See what you have built. See the great oceans and frontiers. See the dynamism and the growth. All can be yours.

The Man leans slightly to one side.

IAGO: Wavering is for the weak. Stand up straight!

The Man does not.

IAGO: I can push you over with a breath. A sigh. A granny could knock you over with her cane. Your impoverished awareness is sickening to me. Stand up straight, before God!

He hunches down into a ball on the ground.

IAGO: I spit on you. Too much humility is a burden. You disgust me. Get up! Get up!

He does not move.

IAGO: I look at you and I see a slave. Your submission does not please me, on the contrary, I see only how easy you are to kill. Be strong, stand, fight! Be a man!

He rises slightly, crouches into a runner's start position.

IAGO: Good. You are low but tensed. Your awareness is taut as your body is. You await the moment to go. Good. Your center of gravity is lowered and your –

The Man raises his arms, cocking them slightly, gesturing outwards towards the audience.

IAGO: Make no appeal! Communication is not of interest to me! I want to feel you. Let me feel your strength. Do not beg for an awareness outside of your own! No! Useless! Stand up again!

He stands up.

IAGO: Now, bark like a dog!

He barks.

IAGO: Louder!

He barks louder.

IAGO: How does it feel to be a dog? Does it feel good? Why did you bark when I told you to? Did you think it would make me happy? No! I don't want a dog, I want a Man! Be a Man!

The Man hangs his head.

IAGO: Pathetic people are so difficult to deal with. What do you accomplish by hanging your head? Will I feel sorry for you? Will I feel sympathy? No, all I see is a wounded Man who won't make it through another winter. Hopelessness. Drudgery. Meat. Yes, be meat. Sink down into the earth, like rotting meat.

He does not move.

IAGO: What, don't you want to be meat? No? Come on, you're meat anyway, act like it!

He does nothing. IAGO pushes him. The Man loses his balance, makes a step, but regains it. IAGO shoves him harder. He falls down.

IAGO: What are you going to do now? Go on, shove me

back! Go on!

The Man sits in a meditation position instead.

IAGO: Oh, meditate! Yes, good! Pretend this isn't happening! Then I can kill your wife and children and you'll still be sitting there telling yourself that it's going to be OK. Isn't that what you want? Isn't it?

MAN: I --

IAGO: What, you can talk? Speak, dog! Speak!

Instead, the Man settles more deeply into his meditation. IAGO sighs, looks at the horizon along with the Man.

IAGO: Yes, look out to the ends of the earth. See the horizon. See yourself sitting there, on that opposite hill there, yes, and see yourself looking at yourself across that distance. You are a mirror, and light. Let the light pass between you, and in the relativistic space between, feel your awareness shift as it rebounds into and out of space. Don't get lost! No, feel it stretch between you. Now, let me try to break that bond.

IAGO: makes a karate chop at the imaginary thread the Man is extending in front of himself. The Man bends slightly with the blow, and twitches.

IAGO: Good, hold onto it! See yourself there, stretched between two poles.

IAGO chops again. The Man cries out, in pain. His eyes snap open.

IAGO: What good did that do you?

MAN: What good are you doing?

IAGO: Oh, you can talk!

MAN: I know what you are.

IAGO: Oh, what am I?

MAN: You're Satan.

IAGO: Ha! Yes, that's a good one. Yes, go on, I'm Satan! That's a great one. Fine, I'm Satan! What are you going to do about it?

MAN: What can I do?

IAGO: I ask the questions here. If I'm Satan, I ask again, what are you going to do about it?

MAN: Who made you Satan?

IAGO slaps him. The Man is stung, looks away.

IAGO: Stop with this question for a question bullshit! *Pause.* God, you're a sniveling idiot. What am I going to do with you? Listen, I'm not Satan. I'm your friend. Look at me. I said, look at me!

He looks.

IAGO: Good. What do you see?

MAN: I see a man.

IAGO: Yes?

MAN: A strong man.

IAGO. laughs.

IAGO: And?

MAN: *Defeated.* And?

IAGO sighs.

IAGO: Lets start from the beginning. Stand up.

The Man stands.

IAGO: Now close your eyes, and touch your nose with the tips of your fingers, like you were trying to get out of another drunk driving charge.

The Man does it.

IAGO: Good, now stand on one leg.

The Man manages, barely.

IAGO: Good, now bark like a dog.

The Man struggles against the order, keeping balance, not barking.

IAGO: I said, Bark!

The Man does not bark.

IAGO: Like this!

IAGO gets right in his face.

IAGO: Arf arf arf arf arf arf arf arf!

The Man loses his balance, stands on both legs again. IAGO goes right on barking, getting louder, and louder. The Man shoves him. IAGO is astonished, smiling.

IAGO: Good, do it again!

The Man shoves him harder.

IAGO: Good, again!

The Man shoves him harder. IAGO falls down.

IAGO: Hit me! Go on!

The Man raises his fist.

IAGO: hissing. Do it, you pussy!

The Man hits IAGO in the shoulder.

IAGO: Ha! Is that all you've got!

IAGO sweeps the Man's legs out from under him, and leaps to his feet. The Man covers his face in his hands.

MAN: I'm worthless.

IAGO: Now, now. It's OK to be worthless. We can take

you to a mental institution. You can make baskets there. It's nice there. You'll be fed, and drugged. There are even pretty girls there who've tried to slit their wrists for a third time, and they're an easy lay because they have no self-esteem at all. They'll spread their legs for anyone, even you. And besides, you're not hard to look at. I'd do you myself, if you weren't physically repugnant to me.

The Man looks up at him.

IAGO: What, did I offend you?

MAN: Yes.

IAGO: Which part? The mental institution? Oh, the easy lay bit? Which?

MAN: Your lack of imagination.

This does piss IAGO off. IAGO start to bark out an insult, but stops himself.

IAGO:
You're more clever than I gave you credit for. Listen, what can you hear? What are people saying about you? Listen!

MAN: No.

IAGO:
Go on, listen! Here's let's see.

IAGO cups his ear.

IAGO: They're saying you're a child molester! Ooh, that's a juicy bit! Little girls turn you on, do they? Or is it little boys? Or both? Do you swing that way? What else? *He cups his ear again.* They're saying you're gay! Well, that's old news. And . . . oh, you're a commie too! You fucking pinko faggot. Go on, say you're a fucking pinko faggot. Say it!

MAN: I . . .

IAGO: Say it! Say you're a gay, pedophiliac communist who likes raping little girls. Say you like buggering them up the −

The Man punches IAGO in the face. IAGO rubs his face, and smiles, wider than ever before.

IAGO: I knew you had it in you.

A very long pause. The Man touches his fist, like he can't quite believe what he did.

IAGO: Now, again.

The Man stands as before.

IAGO:
Humility is a virtue. Be penitent. But not too penitent. See how your head hangs slightly? You submit before a higher authority: God, your neighbors, your elders. You are in equipoise but you have lost the horizon. Look up.

He looks up again.

IAGO: See what you have built. See the great oceans and frontiers. See the dynamism and the growth. All can be yours.

A Marriage Play

A husband and wife stand in the kitchen, where there is a small table and one chair.

MAN: Did you do the dishes?

WOMAN: I thought that was your philosophy.

MAN sits down in the chair.

WOMAN: That's your chair, isn't it?

MAN: I already did the dishes.

WOMAN: I did them!

MAN: No you didn't.

She sits on his lap.

WOMAN: I love you.

MAN: I hate your fucking guts so much. So fucking much. You went to that orgy last night, didn't you. Fucked, what, two, three guys? Did they cum in you?

WOMAN: I love you, honey.

She strokes his face.

MAN: Did you do the dishes?

WOMAN: I did them all, honey. I did them all.

MAN begins to weep. WOMAN stands up.

WOMAN: I live here with you and this is our house and this is our American Dream in the 21st century honey. You know what that means, what with women's empowerment and all, and all our money? I can do whatever the fuck I want and you can't say shit about it.

MAN coughs.

WOMAN: Those are good dishes we have.

MAN: Yeah, they are. I like that pattern you got.

WOMAN: Yeah, what is that pattern?

MAN: The pattern of love, my woman, my one and only woman from somewhere beyond. When I met you in that cafe and you just had to look at me once for me to know I'd found you, and know what are you, some Hollywood whore, some movie star, some bank for the trick I found or you found, and what is this anywhere, you goddamned

SLUT?

And he bursts out of the chair and lurches around the room.

WOMAN: Shhhhh, shhhhh, shh honey. You want to put it in me?

MAN: Not now.

WOMAN: Shhh, I know you do.

MAN: Orgy, orgy, orgy, orgy, porgy, orgy, orgy, orgy, porgy!

WOMAN: Stop it!

MAN: Orgy, orgy, orgy, porgy. You little pneumatic device. With your pumps and your drills and your methods. And your cheap little Los Angeles philosophies.

WOMAN: Shhhhhh, shhhhh, please, shhhhh.

He comes over to her and presses her face between one hand, squeezing her mouth open slightly.

MAN: Shhhhhhh. You're my wife, you know that. You're my wife.

WOMAN: Just fuck me. Just throw me down and fuck me.

MAN watches her for a moment, lets go of her face but steps closer to her.

MAN: You're blind, WOMAN. Blind.

WOMAN starts to cry, and she sits in the chair.

MAN: From out of a dream of music, Los Angeles appears! Glad-handed and dandy, without rhyme or reason, without a name or a face, it's here! Bright as a dime, shiny as a nickel, woven into your hands and into your pants and right into the Louis Vuitton. O Glad Handed Dandies of Santa Monica Boulevard with your Stepchild Wives and Your Ancient Faces and Looters! I sprawl amongst your lot with a wide angle lens and I shit in my boot to feed it to you LIKE A PRINCE!

She laughs, and laughs. and laughs, and laughs, and falls out of the chair, and laughs and laughs and laughs and laughs. And he laughs too, a huge laugh.

WOMAN: Did you do the dishes, honey?

And she laughs.

MAN: I did you, WOMAN. WOMAN, WOMAN, WOMAN from WOMAN, WOMAN of WOMEN, WOMAN of MINE.

WOMAN dances around the stage.

MAN: WOMAN! WOMAN! WOMAN! WOMAN! WOMAN! WOMAN!

And she laughs and spins around and takes off her shirt, and throws it at him and dances around in her skirt and bra.

MAN: Kneel before Zod!

And she crouches down on her hands and knees and crawls towards him.

MAN: Say you're sorry for being a whore.

WOMAN: I'm sorry.

MAN: Say it like you mean it.

WOMAN: I'm sorry for being a whore!

MAN: SAY IT LIKE YOU MEAN IT!

And she grins and crawls closer to him and then kneels in front of him, looking up at him with wide, expectant eyes.

MAN: There you are, girl. There you are.

WOMAN: Here I am.

MAN strokes her face, and she leans into his touch.

WOMAN: What do you want me to do?

MAN: Just look at me.

And she looks at him and he looks down at her for a very long moment. MAN: hums. Hum, hum, hum, hum. And she grows afraid, and her smiling expectant eyes fall away.

MAN: Hmmmmmmmmmmmmmmmmmmmmm. Hmmmmmmmmmmmmmmmmm. HMMMMMMMMMMMMMMMMM!

She grimaces, and looks down at the floor.

MAN: Whale. Hmmmmmmmmmmm. Wasp. Hmmmmmmmmm. Water . . . . . . BIRD!

And she stands and flaps her wings like a leper, lurching about the stage, making horrible noises. And the man smiles.

MAN: Yeah, I LIKE THAT!

She continues to lurch about making odd noises.

MAN: Too much cock, ladies and gentlemen, goes right to the cerebral cortex of the woman! Remember, when preparing for an orgy, get your GLAD HANDED JOHNNY! Get your STAMINA SURPRISE! Psyche yourself up for the LONG NIGHT AHEAD! Go ahead, slurp it up if you want to, it's kosher!

WOMAN: Rrrrrrrrrrrrr ram rod! Rrrrriddle it out pro . . . . fesh . . . .. un . . . . alllllll .. .. . yyyyyyyyyy!

MAN: And if a man loves a woman too much, what then? Does he kill her? Does a man kill his wife for that? Too much love? Where else would I go without you? Find another ingenue I don't love? One I can fit into the taxi and stuff into my boxes?

WOMAN: I'm too much for you, aren't I?

MAN goes to sit in chair again.

MAN: Maybe, maybe.

WOMAN: And what if you were me, hmmmm? Some pretty girl lost in Los Angeles, scooped up and put on parade for her tits and ass and sexy voice? Locked away in a big bright cage and brought out to be watered like a good horse? What if you were me, watching your body die, and your future children die in your mind, in this dark city of ours, where would you go but up into the hills to take off your clothes and forget who you are? What do you think is up in those hills, honey? Forgiveness? I go up there to forget you, forget myself, forget this whole fucking century! I don't want to remember anything!

MAN: Maybe, maybe.

WOMAN: And then maybe you remember something, some detail, lost in the pleasure dome with the onlookers greedy and wise, some look the young man had for the young woman next to you, a way he didn't look at you, a way he'll never look at you anymore, but you still look at me that way, you see? You still look at me that way!

And she rolls up in a ball on the floor and curls up and rocks herself back and forth. And the MAN gets up and prods her with his foot, circling around her.

MAN 2 enters, an older man.

MAN 2: Hey, hey, hey, Mr. and Mrs. Wallace, glad you could make it!

MAN: George.

MAN 2: I love it. I love it! Tell me more!

MAN: George. My wife and I are afraid. What's happening in Hollywood?

MAN 2: George! George!

MAN: You're George, stop it.

MAN 2: Georgie, Georgie, I bought you a ticket!

MAN: I'm George, aren't I?

MAN 2: George Wallace! Bright in the sky and pretty as a penny, give me some skin, motherfucker!

MAN: gives him skin.

WOMAN keeps whimpering, lying on the floor.

MAN 2: I'm George too. Hey, you know what I heard the other day? Susan Sarandon bought a big ranch somewhere out near Modesto and she's gonna raise new chickens! You know what a new chicken is? It's a bullet from a fucking gun, fucker! You get a new chicken from me, you're fucked forever!

MAN: Susan Sarandon did that?

MAN 2: Man, I love her in that cult flick with that tight little body of hers! What is that flick, that cult flick?

MAN: The Raising of the Dead Stones.

MAN 2: No, no, not that one, that one sucks, what's the one with Tim Curry where he's an insane person?

MAN: That's every movie with Tim Curry, george.

MAN 2: DON'T YOU EVER CALL ME GEORGE.

MAN: Sorry, George, I mean, sir.

WOMAN gets up from the ground and goes to embrace MAN 2, not letting go.

WOMAN: The Rocking Horse Picture Show.

MAN 2: God I love rocking horses. I used to ride one as a kid, rock back and forth on that mother, just grind away at it all hours of the night when the kids were asleep, I'd just go down into the basement and rock on that mother and call it my favorite names and I'd stroke it's plastic skin, and it's like me now, you know, me in this city and I'm growing older and I've got your wife, right here, right here in my arms forever and I can do what I need to with her, you know that? That's the deal you made, isn't it? Isn't that the deal you made George?

MAN: Don't call me George.

MAN 2: Yes sir, Mr. Wallace!

WOMAN: Yes sir, Mr. Wallace!

MAN 2: I made you what you are. I made you and I made your wife. And I can take it all away in a heartbeat. You remember that little 17 year old you had all those years back? That little high school girl you just couldn't resist?

WOMAN: Not that story again!

MAN 2: The statute of limitations isn't up yet, Georgie!

Not quite yet, not quite yet by a long shot. Rape is a serious charge.

MAN: I know, Mr. Wallace.

WOMAN: Mr. Wallace! Mr. Wallace! Mr. Wallace! Mr. Wallace makey the biggy buckeroonies!

MAN 2: Woman here tells me you've been remiss in your husbandly duties. Haven't been doing the business.

WOMAN: Awww, he does the business real good!

MAN: Yeah, I do the business real good.

MAN 2: Sure you do, Mr. Wallace! That's what I can count on you for! To do the business! How about you do another bit of business for me? How about you kill a man?

WOMAN: Kill him! Kill him! Kill him, honey! Rape his ass!

MAN 2: Now now, little sugar. You behave yourself. Daddy has a treat for you later.

MAN: I paid what I owe.

MAN 2: This isn't about the money, Mr. Wallace. Mr. Wallace says you have to pay in kind, now. Pay in all kinds.

MAN: She pays for me.

MAN 2: Sure she does, Georgie. We all know that. But she's getting a little long in the tooth now, don't you think? And we like them fresh up in the hills. Real nice and fresh,

Hollywood style. So fresh you can smell it from a hundred yards. A fresh face.

MAN: You son of a bitch.

WOMAN: I'm still nice and fresh! I am!

MAN: I know you are, honey. You'll always be young to me, you know that.

WOMAN puts back on her shirt.

MAN 2: Georgie, Georgie, a romantic! I love that about you! You remember that restaurant we ate at last week with those bigwigs from Switzerland with what's her face, the black chick with the huge ass?

MAN: She's Persian, George.

MAN 2: Whatever! The restaurant!

—

And we are at the restaurant. And they all clap! The waiter brings two more chairs for the party of three.

WOMAN: Shhhhhhhhhhh. It's the magic hour.

They are seated.

MAN 2: I love this restaurant.

WAITER: Today we have the blood of the newlywed, fresh from the vein, with overtones of licorice and honey, and a touch of fennel. Also highly recommended we have the death of an old city, or the death of a young one, your choice! And I bring you lamb's heads and merchants of yore, soft to the palate, rich with time and frankincense, all ablaze in your mind for a final tragedy!

WOMAN: I'll have the beef!

Scene 2

Waiter: (*to MAN 2*) And for you, sir?

MAN 2: What's the special?

WAITER: I'm glad you asked, Mr. Wallace. Mr. Wallace in back has prepared something special for our loyal customers. Everyone loves it, real good. They love it so good they can taste it in the back of their mouths for hours, Mr. Wallace, like a sore that won't heal and keeps bleeding into your mouth, like money, Mr. Wallace, it tastes like old New York money, like old Persian money, like gold, Mr. Wallace, like God.

MAN 2: Sounds pretty good. What's in it? It's not shrimp is it? I hate shrimp.

WAITER: It goes down easy, for a man of your temperament and maturity, Mr. Wallace, may I call you George?

MAN 2: Sure, go ahead, I've only been coming here 10 minutes!

WAITER: 10 minutes is a long time in this town, Mr. Wallace, you know that. A long time.

WOMAN: I love beef!

MAN 1: You got a hamburger and freedom fries?

WOMAN: I love freedom fries!

WAITER: We've got a lot of fried freedom fries here, little woman. Kinds like you wouldn't believe. i mean, Los Angeles is a world city. The world's here, watching us, watching us in our sun-swept squalor. I know you can't believe it, being a woman, but men work in this town, for women like you. Women like you who come in here like princesses and order up the big surprise, or maybe only an expensive salad, and we know your looks and we know your tastes and we know when to shut you down like a tramp and give you the Really Big Order, and I'm talking about the REally Big Order, straight from God, Mr. Producer is Listening, Mrs. Wallace, and he knows you've been a GOOD GIRL!

WOMAN: I have?????

MAN: Sure you have, honey.

MAN 2: She's been a good girl!

WAITER: You're going onto the A list real fucking soon!

WOMAN starts to tear up.

WOMAN: Really?

MAN 1: Finally, really?

MAN 2: I talked to them about it, Mr. Wallace, she's waited her turn, and we've decided if we give her a couple Academy Awards and invite her to the Big Palm Springs Party this winter she might, she might just make it ONTO THE A LIST!

WAITER: Mr. Wallace here is correct about one thing. She waited her turn.

WOMAN: What do you know, sir? I want your beef! I mean, I want my beef!

WAITER: Your beef is coming, Mrs. Wallace. You've waited this long, can't you wait another month, another year, anotehr century? This city has waited a long tiem for the coming of a woman of your caliber, woman, with those eyes of yours from beyond, ready to raze a city to the moon and stamp out its life with your cunt, you think you've got that in you? Can you fire a gun into a man's face without flinching? Can you cry in the night when nobody's watching? Can you fuck like a bunny? Can you dance like nobody's watching? Can you still dream? CAN YOU STILL DREAM, WOMAN?

WOMAN: Get me my beef!

WAITER: Coming right up.

MAN 2: This is an eccentric waiter. Don't worry, I know him, he's a friend.

MAN 1: Yeah, he's definitely a friend.

WOMAN: You know this restaurant, honey?

MAN: Yeah, I think I came here once before with Mr. Wallace here. A while back. Had the fish. Maybe an omelet. It was a good time. Always nice to get out in the afternoon, hobnob a little and rub shoulders. it's a good town if you know how to live in it. I do all right. I follow most fo the orders. I got the house. I got the wife. I got that gun in the closet. And the other one in the basement. And i got the shotgun they made me kill my dog with, making me watch me kill that dog on video and laughing, and I got a girl somewhere too, can't even remember her name, but it's a good life, goddamn, I love the fish here!

WOMAN: I hate fish. It stinks.

MAN 2: How is your little girl?

MAN: (*crying.*) I don't know. I don't know.

WOMAN: You have a little girl?

MAN 2: She's fine, Mr. Wallace. You know that. She's being taken care of, company style. Nothing too dramatic, just an upgrade here or there. You know, a little warp drive for the younger generation. She's a feisty one.

WOMAN: You never told me you had a daughter, George! George, are you OK?

MAN: NO.

WOMAN: What's the matter?

MAN: Maybe I should leave.

MAN 2: You can't leave yet, George, the first course hasn't even arrived.

WOMAN: Rome, O Rome! I want to go back!

MAN 2: You can never leave Rome!

WOMAN: Oh but it's been so long! And lost the Prada jacket I got there, I think some bitch stole it! I looked all over for it, but I couldn't find it. My favorite jacket, gone! And my earrings too, my earrings from Rome, honey, you remember those?

MAN 2: You can never leave Rome!

Waiter comes back.

WAITER: You can never leave Rome!

WOMAN: Where's my beef?

WAITER: It's coming right up! Can I get you folks anything else while you wait? Some live music? A live frog?

WOMAN: You know, I did the dishes today! All by myself!

WAITER: I know you did, Mrs. Wallace! We're very proud of you. We have it on videotape. You're sterile, Mrs. Wallace.

They all look at the waiter.

WAITER: Just kidding, Mrs. Wallace, I'm a kidder.

WOMAN starts to cry.

MAN 1 comforts her.

MAN 1: Shhh, honey. Shhhh. We'll have a baby, I promise.

WAITER: Once I had a baby, I put it in the road, and laughed when heard a crunchy, from where some tires goed!

MAN 2: That's a good one! I like that.

MAN: You hear that one about two whores in a box? They fought their way out with a pinochle stick.

WOMAN: What's that mean?

MAN 2: They took a risk. You gotta take a risk in life, you wanna succeed. That's what I did.

WOMAN: (*to MAN 2.*) I love you, Georgie!

MAN 2: I love you so much my heart aches. My tears flow. And I saw my aunt Marie, floating in the chicken soup. Where did you go, Aunt marie, all those years ago? You vanished into thin air. Was it Hollywood that did it to you? The Mob? I wish I remembered your name. Lost into the vasty deep, like my soul, like my iron grasp, like my hope.

WOMAN: I like how you talk. Do you have a rock hard cock every morning?

MAN 2: Hard like a diamond every morning at 7am!

MAN: Like hell you do, you old fart.

MAN 2: My erections stand the test of time, like an obelisk in the desert, it stands for strength, for union, for The Act of Uniformity! Are you uniform, Mr. Wallace?

MAN: Where is my uniform?

WOMAN: I love you in uniform, Georgie!

MAN 1 gets up and does an elaborate, slow dance with the Waiter.

WAITER: Where's the beef?

MAN 1: Beef. beef.

WAITER: Where's my lingo?

MAN 1: Write it down, man!

WAITER: I wrote it down, I wrote it down on my hand and forgot about it.

WOMAN: Don't do that, honey!

MAN 1: I wrote it down, I wrote it down, I wrote it down, I wrote it down in Hollywood!

MAN 2: IN HOLLYWOOD?????

MAN: In Hollywood!

WAITER: In Hollywood!

WOMAN: O Hollywood, you with your many skies and your many agents! Rip me a new dress so I can flock like a maze into the back of the restaurant and fuck the right sous chef who will make me millions!

WAITER: We have a good one right here, his name is Samuel Beckett!

WOMAN: Is he hot?

WAITER: Smoking hot, ma'am, but you have to pay him.

MAN 2: O Hollywood, you with your Man Petrochemical Arms! Hold me tight! Hold me tight! *he weeps.*

MAN 1 and Waiter continue their odd dance.

WAITER: I've seen your daughter, Mr. Wallace!

MAN 1 continues to dance.

WAITER: You know she's only 14?

MAN 1: I know how old my daughter is, asshole.

WAITER: She's moving up in the world! Got a nice body and a pretty face and she knows how to sing! God, you should hear her sing.

MAN 1: I'm going to rip your throat out with my car keys.

WAITER: O Hollywood! You here, in Hollywood! Tell me something, mr. wallace, what did you think when you came here? Was it love?

WOMAN: Love!

MAN 2 becomes sick and curls up on the floor.

Waiter stands over MAN 2.

WAITER: Arma virumque! You with your many lives and hands! Where will you carry your father? You didn't make it to Rome, did you? You died on the way! AHHAHAHA-HAHAHHAHAHAHAHAHAHAH!

WOMAN: HAHAHHAHAHAHAHAHHAHAHAHA!

MAN 1 attacks waiter and they sprawl on the ground.

WOMAN: AHAHAHHAHAHAHHAHAAHH!

MAN 2 gets up and lurches abuput the stage.

MAN 2: HOLLYWOOD. Oh, God. I feel sick. Hollywood! Hollywoodland, where did you go? Where are you going? I'm gopign to die . . . I'm going to die . . . . . FEED ME!

Waiter takes out a butter knife and holds it like a gun and blows MAN 1 away.

WOMAN: AHHHHHHHHHHHHHHHH!

MAN 2: I knew it had to happen sooner or later. He knew too much.

WOMAN: What did you do to my husband?

Waiter grins and sits in the chair.

WAITER: Come here, sit in my lap.

MAN 2 stands over MAN 1

MAN 2: Your daughter will be fine, George. I'll take care of her.

MAN 1 sprawls into a crouched position, and groans.

WOMAN: I need a new man!

WAITER: I'm right here, lover. I may be poor, but I'm going places.

WOMAN: What will we do for money?

WAITER: I'll wait tables by day and steal cars by night. And I'll sneak into people's houses and photograph them asleep. And I'll install cameras in their daughter's bedrooms and videotape their orgies for blackmail purposes, and Hollywood will love, O Hollywood will love, O Hollywood will love their light and might into a smile in the dark bright day in the middle of Vine, wrenching it out into a Pink Flamingo, dancing in the street with so much blood, can you see it?

WOMAN: No!

WAITER: It's a musical, you see, the dead whores and the intelligentsia and the pinko faggot dreamers, lost in the bright day-night, looking for the way out of the forest, and there is NO WAY OUT! it's hilarious!

WOMAN: I guess it's funny!

Meanwhile, MAN 1 has crawled over to the chair, and is trying to dislodge the couple from their position.

MAN 2 gets a phone call.

MAN 2: Yes, we're here. I know I need the beef. Yes, it's good beef. Spicy. Expensive? Well, how much? Mexico is listening. Yes? No, not yet. Well, all right.

MAN 1: (*still dying.*) Who was that?

MAN 2: Mexico says we need to leave. They need the restaurant.

WOMAN: Is Chapo coming?

MAN 2: Chapo??

MAN 1: I hate Chapo.

WAITER: Chapo is a good man to love! He of the Man Ak-47s and grenades! he of the Man bright children, sprawled somewhere in the green jungle, dreaming of Apocalypse.

WOMAN: Do we really have to go?

MAN 2: I don't know. It would seem wise.

MAN 1 lurches to his feet.

MAN 1: Chapooooooooo! Chapooooooooo! I need you. I need you, MAN. What do I do now? WHAT DO I DO

NOW?

WOMAN: You know Chapo?

MAN 1: I dream about him at night, with his light and his darkness, and his armies marching through alleys and through winding doors. He took my daughter away from me.

MAN 2: Chapo the Kidnapper!

WOMAN: He was made by Bush One, you know? Bush the Broccoli Hater of the Long heroin Knives! he of the Parachute and the Next Dimension! He of the DEA and the Dramamine! Pack up your weapons and mine your swords! Chapo is coming for us all!

MAN 2: Shut up, woman. Chapo is happy down in Mexico. He just wants us to get out of this restaurant. It's going to blow up.

WOMAN: Chapo is a mad bomber now?

MAN 1: Chapo. Chapo. I need you, **MAN:**. Give me back my phone!

MAN 2: I told you I was here.

MAN 2 hands MAN 1 the phone.

MAN 1: Answer, answer, answer.

Waiter becomes Chapo, standing straight and narrow. They stand at opposite sides of the stage.

MAN 1: Chapo! Where is my fucking daughter?

CHAPO: I have her safe, hombre. Safe as houses. Safe as your house, up in the hills. You like that house, don't you? Dark Dreamer? What was it you told me back in the early 80s? No Borders Anymore, Just Landscapes! Just AI Landscapes, stretching out into Eternity? Your daughter is there too, you see? She's not even human anymore! She's mine and she's yours and she's ours, and she's fighting for her fucking life every moment at the age of 14! She might even be a Jew by now! Rhyming her deep words with the Hebrew and the missions statements and the media training! Go on, ask me a question!

MAN 1: Who was it hurt you?

CHAPO: My mother.

MAN 1: Reds, greens, blues, whole fucking rainbow.

CHAPO: Justine's harassing me.

FROM OFF-STAGE: AND STOP! THIS SHOW IS OVER! Evacuate the cafe now. This is an order from the United States government, brought to you by Coca Cola.

CHAPO: But I'm not done talking yet.

WOMAN: Go on, ask me a question.

MAN 1: Where will we be in ten years?

WOMAN: If you follow orders, you too can be part of the Economic Evacuation. Bet against the dollar, bet against the yen, bet against the euro, bet for the Ruble! Bet for the terrorist enterprise! Bet for Al Qaeda and the shining light of Apocalypse! O Moon River with your Red Heifer and your shiny lights! Come to us in Wall Street in the night so we can see you blowing and take us up into he stars where well be new people, different from the ones we are now, different, O SO DIFFERENT? This is America! Stand up and give me 20!

And they do jumping jacks.

WOMAN: She counts off. One! two three! Etc.

At twenty, WOMAN starts to do jumping jacks and MAN 1 inspects the troops.

MAN 1: Are you ready for a civil war? Are you ready to die for your country?

WOMAN: Which country is it?

MAN 2: The country of the Jews?

WOMAN: Israel?

MAN 1: Israel is Man countries, a country of the mind. Think of it, Jews in space! Faster, I say faster! How are your weapons caches?

ALL: Strong!

MAN: Are you ready to fight?

ALL: No!

MAN: Are you ready to run?

ALL: Yes!

MAN: Run, then, run for your lives!

They let out small, weak screams and run vaguely in a circle around the stage.

MAN 1: Let me tell you a story. I was young once. I saw the pretty women in the street and the bars back in the 70s and it was still free love then, you know, sex was like shaking hands, and you could get the clap and maybe the syph, but nothing too nasty. And I remember the mad bombers and the hijackings and OPEC and the long low light of love that streamed from Carter the Peanut-man's face, he of the Lustful Thoughts, and I thought, we're actually getting somewhere. This country is going to collapse and we can have a new government, maybe a new fascist government like in Nazi GerMan, or maybe a new peaceful hippie collective like in Ecotopia, or maybe just a whole lot of roving gangs, which is what Chapo wants now, and the good old Military-Industrial-Congressional-Entertainment complex. I remember the lights of neon at night and the miniskirts and the crazy hair and the blues and the dawn of Rap, and I remember the look on my daughter's face in 1999, right before the Millenium. And I remember you too, Old Dreamers! I remember your slow lapse into ExPatriating and Secession!

ALL: Manhattan-Versailles Secedes!

MAN 1: O The Secession! O the broken dream! They tried it in 1774 and 1779 and 1863 so why not get it right this time? Just cut Manhattan-Versailles off like Florida in the Bugs Bunny animation and float out into the Atlantic?

WOMAN: I want to say something.

MAN 1: Yes, honey?

WOMAN: How much money can I make out of this deal?

MAN 1: How much do you want?

WOMAN: A lot! A lot a lot!

MAN 1: How much is a lot a lot?

WOMAN: 500 million? 2 billion?

MAN 1: How about .. . . 42 Zwolfillion?

MAN 2 and WAITER She's a Zwolfillionaire!

MAN 1: You'll get a network and a brain implant and you can be Tally Isham or President of the United States or a Terrorist Leader or a World Reknowned Porn Star with agents in every land, and your own space shuttle, and in a few years, your own dome on Mars! When the aliens come you can bow down to them in your senescence and recite their Man languages and receive their tentacles into your mouth and be free! Think of it! Tentacles Against Your Teeth and You're Free! Just set it all on fire, right? Like you set me on fire, like your cunt sets me on fire.

WOMAN: You always say the sweetest things, honey. And she hangs off his arm.

Waiter and MAN 2: A Zwolfillionaire!

WOMAN: What will I do with all that money? 4, 2 with 42 zeroes!

MAN 1: Man, honey. You're gonna be rich.

WOMAN: RICH!

Waiter and MAN 2: (*deadpan.*) Rich. Rich as Croesus.

WOMAN: I'm gonna get a new car and a new vagina and a new face and new tits and a new Lear Jet and a new Island in the Pacific! Tavalu shall be mine along with Madagascar and New England! Brittany and Monaco shall be mine, along with Transylvania and Westphalia! Outer Mongolia shall be mine, and the Ides of March! I want Caesar destroyed! And i shall rule with an Iron Hand and a soft, spiked whip! And all citizens shall be revoked from their lives with their zits and their incontinence and their inconsequence. Acceptable losses, collateral damage, reasonable externalities, an appropriate decay rate? What is your decay rate, soldiers?

MAN 1: We're not your soldiers, woman.

WOMAN: Yes, you are! I'm a Zwolfillionaire now! I molest you with my mind and cunt and my smallest movement of my lips or little toe makes cities tremble!

MAN 1: You're a nutcase, honey. Let's just go home and fuck and we'll give you your medication.

WAITER: Zwolfillionnnaire, Zwolfillionaire, what Rex gets your hex wet?

WOMAN: I like it!

MAN 2: She likes it. It's good for her. it's psychotropic medication. It eases the mind and greases the soul for the afterlife!

WOMAN: I like it!

MAN 1: Come on, let's get out of here.

MAN 2: I'll come with you! This place is dead anyway.

WAITER: We remember your faces! Come back! We serve you the food and you pay!

WOMAN: Bye bye!

Waiter exits.

WOMAN: sits on the stairs.

WOMAN: Mmmm I'm sleepy.

MAN 2: So who gets to fuck her first?

MAN 1: Let's get her her medication first, George.

MAN 2: I need her now.

WOMAN: I'm ready!

MAN 1: I need her now too.

WOMAN: I hate you all day long, with my head between my legs.

MAN 2: Don't hate your husband so much. He's an obedient servant.

WOMAN: I hate you so much, honey, all day long!

MAN 1: I hate you too, honey. I love the pattern you chose for the dishes.

WOMAN: You do?

MAN 2: Come on into the bedroom.

MAN 2 and WOMAN exit.

MAN 1: Daughter! Daughter! Daughter! Daughter! Daughter! Be strong daughter! I love you! I love you, daughter! I love you! Daughter. Why did I leave you, daughter . . . Daughter, be strong for me. Be strong for your Daddy. I'll come to get you, honey. I'll come to get you. And we'll get out of here.

I am Chumash, I am Aching

She walks through the noonday crowds, threading along the city sidewalk.

I am Chumash I am aching. I am aching I am Chumash. I am twenty-five years old. I live near the sea. I live in a city, the city of the Queen.

My Queen! Listen! I am coming for you!

The monarchy they say is never ending. We all want the royal blood. Even I do. Even I who hate all royals want their blood inside me, the woman in me wants the king's seed, and I want him dead, at once, I am mantis and Persephone, the pomegranate is inside my womb but I want to chew the head—

I cannot leave. I cannot leave the city. I cannot leave.

I am Chumash and I ache, with the sea inside my brain.

Under the world the world under the world the world under the world our world Indian and African the tree the hill the river and the sea, the ocean is a quiver of the sun and I will find the key inside your barricaded room, Queen! Queen of the Angels! Queen of the Holy Messengers! I bear you a message from our Regency! The Revolution is inside you.

When I was a girl I was apartment people and I knew that I was Indian but I knew I was a subject of the Queen and in her gracious liberty I could be saved.

And now here we are!

Now here we are. Apartment people with our pennies in our pockets and our hands upon the bar—I like it here, I do. Have you never seen it? We Chumash know the queens come and go, but I want them gone, you see? I want us to remember.

I want us to remember the ocean. The most terrifying thing, freedom. To swim, anywhere you want to.

Each of us her messenger! I am her messenger and so are you! Even if you didn't know you are an angel, you are an angel! For an angel is only a messenger! We're no more divine than rocks, or suns. We're no more divine than these words out of my mouth.
Each of us the Queen's Messenger! And her message is simple: she is queen. Everything you do, you do for her.

This is fair and easy and it is right, we serve and we are glad to serve because we love it, because it is good, because it makes us happy: to know that together, with her love, we are mighty and cannot fall, the city of the Chumash the city of ten million messengers is One, it is united.

The hive of ants. The swirling ocean.

I say, each of is a messenger. I say, down with the queen.

I say, down with the queen!

Off with her head!

Oh, off her with head!

Off with the Queen's head!

I say, off with the Queen's head!

I say, off with the Queen's head!

I say, off with her head!

I say, off with her head!

Off with the head of the Queen!

—

Write me a story, messenger! Write me a story!

Once, up in the trees, the mother and the father cried into the night to summon home the hunting children. And their teeth crunched through the insects and they slept inside their burrow in the tree.

And the mother, little sharp toothed nocturnal jungle mammal, all two inches tall, she is queen too, isn't she?

Is it only efficiency of communication, this royalty obsession? Must warring Nature always abhor an empty throne up at the top?

We need the proper metaphor.

James Bond is a messenger. But can't James be cool and tight and long and loved and bold and hurt and lost and wild in the night without England?

Without the Queen?

Can't James be James without England? Did he ever need England, really?

Don't we all want to be like James? Don't I want to be the Bond Girl?

I've got my laser beam, I've got my boobs! I fight for you!

—

But you have to see inside the city, see inside its heart. See inside its old dark heart. Just burrowed in the heart of the jungle. Timing with our teeth for a little insect hunting.

She lunges a little, biting with her teeth.

Inside the dark heart of the city you are waiting. Who is it? Who is here? Who has done this? What warrior has despoiled my throne? Who has burnt down my forest? What hunter is awilding unto my breast?

For I am a woman and as I want the king's seed Persephone inside my womb Demeter in my brain the teeth inside my mouth will crush the hope that we can separate the Queen from out our worshipful faces, from out our worshipful hands.

For the Queen is us and she shows us us, for the Queen is us and she shows us us all, and we worship ourselves, we worship ourselves. Here we messengers deliver the message: we are here! Oh, we are here. Here we messengers deliver the message, Oh, we are here!

But if everyone is an angel, if every messenger of this City of the Queen were to arm their words which is to arm their minds with the message: not to kill the Queen, no.

No, not kill her. Not kill her, no. Kill the queen but not the woman. Kill the idea.

I want to kill the idea! How can you kill an idea! Help me, help me. Help me kill it.

We must kill it.

I am bond girl, I Chumash, I ask for aid, m'aidez, ajuyete me, we must crush the crown to dust.

See inside the heart of the city.

Look inside your mother's heart. Look inside your mother's heart. Look inside:

Would you have your men be only means? Would you have your sisters be only enemies? Mother, mother, the

Queen is hungry, why must we keep feeding her?

Democracy theocracy autocracy thalossocracy. Thalossocracy old soul, the Meridian wine the sword the feral mad entwined with thee, thalossocrat! Thalossocrat of Athens!

In Echo Park, Thallosocrat of Athens! Gerontocrat, elite.

Bow before the Queen of the Angels! Bow before the City's Queen!

Ajuyute me, the crown it hurts my head, it hurts your head—

Democracy, democracy—

Build me a city, star!

Build me a city underneath the city! For every day a thousand years, for every weight a thousand weights, for every dawn, no light!

Fill me a city with the poor, fill me a city with hands! Fill me a city with the long low light of heart-rending love, chipped slow into the bridge of the pontifex, built over, built over again, the Greek and Roman arch made slow and loving under every branch, but the Pontifex shall serve the queen!

And over standing by the Bridge, the Pontchardon, the Pinkerton, the bridge guardian, long strong arm of the Queen, so shall the churl fear the night and the Chumash fear the white, but in the city of the churls, which star you build me, what you build me is us all again: this ache, this ache of insect in my mouth, the cicada sound and the cicada oil, glistening, we fear to hunt without our broad totem standing down to view us and our human bridge of souls kept all to founder into sea—

For the arm of the many twined arm Universe is long—

And the arm of the Pontifex is long! Your arm is long, man! Your foot is strong! Kneel and be a bridge for me, over the water! Build me a bridge over the sea!

And it shall happen.

But why can we not sway into ourselves and make religious energy with all our might for us and all why must it be only for the Queen!

Queens Priests and Oligarchs and Lords! Out of the Wheat the Lord and out of the Lord, Is all the bloody bloodied blooding wars of us.

Help me build a city, girl, my little thalossocrat, every good girl loves a sailor and every good boy does fine above the violining breeze so play for me the winter night and play for me the fire, and play for me the holy spirit nuclear and white the brightest kite that shines out over this our Chumash ocean spiriting fine and mad so mad to gleam the greater vastness of its dreaming—

Build me a city, girl! Chumash and Lords!

Washington where is your cherry tree! I have it in my twat!

My twat is dangerous!

My twat's inside the sea—

My Queen, religious energy to you the great Vagina and
your so vast unfolding is a mutant horror of gods avatars
and deities unnumbered, numberless, your vagina is so vast
that I must just be bacteria swimming in its fecund immensity, another Pinkerton, guardian of the holiest of bridges,
the birth canal—

Pontifex, build me a bridge over the Chumash sea!

Pontifex! I need that bridge! Stat!

Build me a bridge over the sea!

Martin! Luther! You whose name means people's warrior!
I need that bridge over the sea! North Sea or West it makes
no difference, man! Give me an arch show me where to
mark the stone and trim the mortar.

Here in this life.

Not the next life, but this one!

Not the next life, but this!

World without end but not amen! In this life!

World without end and in this unending Primordial soup of
sea the universe can see the meaning of our acts we do not
need divinity to elapse the breaking of our deep's desire:
only to be and change, and in this changing we must be fair,
we must let so much go—

We must let so much go. The bridge over the sea. The
mighty ocean. The name Chumash. Even my gender:

woman, it too goes away at last, over some billion year arc.

For the many twined arm of the universe is long but it bends—

———

Martin, London Bridge is Falling!

Martin, I am Bond Girl!

I am Messenger and my message is: I'm hot. Pick up the phone and dial. Pick up the phone and dial. Call home—call home—

Phone home across the sky—

I am Messenger so come with me the city says, I wear the holy reeds, my Marathon will run, so run, I bear the fruit and I hone the axe and my message is: I last, so run with me, but can't you see, we are all running anyway!

We will outrun the sun, Martin! We will outrun the sun! The Chumash are laughing in their casino!

Ranchero! Make me a movie.

Ranchero! How do the kine today?

I smell a stampede in the air, ranchero, ranchero, hold me.

Make me a movie! Make me move! Throw a nickel in my hat!

Martin, how fast does the many-twined of the universe

bend towards justice? Is it fast enough to save me?

Martin. But I am woman, eh? Women are recoverable, if young, from any disaster, and this is why we long for the Queen, and hate her—

Call home across the air and make the city flat. Arrange the melody and drop the act, reality TV is here to say: it's you. We're here for you. This is you. Hold the mirror and sharpen the axe it'll hurt but only for a minute, we need to implant the crown beneath the skin, the royal destiny is feared but it is doable, so do it for the stars, just do it for the stars.

—

Producer, climb over the wall for me! Producer, tell me my phone number! Hold me in the Model T, Producer, let me see inside the city's heart.

—

Make me a movie for thalossocracy. Every good girl loves a sailor and every good girl likes missiles fired on South Asia so make a good movie for thalossocracy and make it good, the billboards are there we need to use them, Ladybird likes it real tasty fine; she was from Texas and they like billboards!

But anyway, what's the story, hey? It's all about the story. The killing of the queen. The idea inside your head. Not the body but the crown, the woman is recoverable from any disaster but the tiara must be destroyed.

Take off that princess costume, girly! No more pretty princesses! Go to your quinceañera in blue jeans! Show off your ass!

Kill the Queen inside.

she sits down on a wall.

I don't remember, I don't remember any more. Why I started. What was I doing. The city of messengers is so full of messages I feel like it's gonna explode. They keep us boiling, testing the valve, but it gets so goddamned hot—

But nobility is in some ways only comparison, the precise instantiation artificially of some natural divisions, but difference is not hierarchical.

Am I more beautiful than you? Are you taller? Am I dumber? Can you run faster? Can you remember more? Can you, God help us, keep your mouth shut?

I don't remember. I don't remember who I was.

And the Queen too is this destiny of Nature, to compare, and to weigh. Is it more efficient than democracy, this eternal kingship queenship lords and lordings?

It's not polite to compare but Nature ain't polite, pick the prettiest girl you see and marry her, carry her away, to the Tower, to the Tower of Pain, to the Tower of Destiny, O Make me Princess—

I've got a glass slipper up my ass. It's gonna break.

Keep your legs moving, girl!

She gets up and walks again.

Once upon a time the people came under the oaks. And up in the oaks they could see the stars, and later they lay them down into the sidewalk.

Under the oaks we're safe. And the acorn keeps body and soul together, and the stars beneath the sidewalk keep the dream alive, of princesses and kings.

Where do we keep the princesses and kings? Why do we want them so much, Producer? Why am I she, and not the braunen augen on the opposite platform?

Cabbages and Kings and merry wings.

Lovers forts and savages, games and thrones and musical wings, tragedy and ignorance aside, it makes for a nice story, doesn't it? The evil stepmother and the beauty kept inside, in her burka, waiting for the Princeling to draw his Excalibur and deliver the nuclear winter, isn't that how it goes? I need a working theory!

—

Producer, pitch me!

—

The Producer appears.

Producer: What if we kill the Queen in the middle of the street! With a genuine Jalisco band playing!

Chumash Girl: No, no, we're not killing her!

Producer: We execute her in public, and throw her head into the sewer! Or put it on a pike and parade with it in the street, with everybody singing!

Chumash Girl: I kind of like that one.

Producer: You see, the Blood is Divine! It delivers us from grace and into mortality! It completes the circle of our brief lives!

Chumash: We keep the woman alive. But we kill the Queen.

Producer: This, this is not good theater, no. Democracy is not good theater!

Chumash: Isn't it?

Producer: Isn't it?

Chumash: Kiss me.

Producer: No, not yet.

Chumash: Kiss me, Producer.

He kisses her.

Chumash: I need a working theory.

Producer: You're a good kisser.

Chumash: Why isn't democracy good theater?

Producer: Where is the drama?

Chumash: Everywhere. The kingdom.

Producer: I don't know.

Chumash: It's your turn. I'm tired of talking.

Producer: No, no, come on.

Chumash: Come on, Producer, I'm not kidding.

Chumash girl takes the camera and points it at Producer.

Chumash: (*From behind camera.*) Let's see what ya got!

—

Producer: I am Anglo-Saxon. I am a man. I am thirty-four years old. I live in the city of the Chumash, Our Lady the Queen, she of so many messengers, what does she need so many messengers for?

Constant war, constant fear, it's depressing. Fuck the angels. They're only messengers for the king and queen, god in heaven on his throne. We need better metaphors. Metaphors for democracy. We need to escape these goddamned Middle Ages.

Maybe technology will actually help! My word a door, my hand, amplified a thousand times with evil little implants, to know my every whim, I'm a king, but I'm just a guy with a lot of little robots, same as you, empowered but not overpowering.

I am Anglo-Saxon, I came over the sea. In my bark were books, stories of the war, stories of the winter, of the cave, stories of the monsters in the trees, and the warrior men and women lusting in their hearts and thirsting in their veins for meaning, for a word—

What is the logos, what is the word? Give me a word, brother. Give me a word. Will you give me a word? To the wise or to the ordinary or to the stupid. Give me a word like giving me a hand, and Puck makes the amends but each of these peace treaties with Nature is bought from them, like from the Chumash and their cousins, the treaties and the handshakes are only searches for more weapons, we need the word, we need the word to say, only this much, and only this time, I am yours, but not until tomorrow, only for today, for it is this life, it is this life.

If I am king then kill me, if I am revolutionary, kill me, if I am citizen, then kill me, for a city needs Pinkertons and our bridges need no guards, we need no guards for our bridges. Once you cross, often, you cannot go back anyway.

No, let me be a man, won't you? Won't you let me be a man?

For the Jews the Beginning was a Word and for the Christians the Word became Flesh but either is useful insofar as they're limited delimiting systems. Neither eternal, neither divine.

But the world is eternal.

The terrible puzzle of the interstellar dark is not its immensity but the fragility of starfaring races: we suppose that we will not survive as a unified and loving and enduring people, long enough, to cross that dark, those many darks, and meet the others like us, and share a word or two with the aliens.

So it is not distance but love that divides us. But if the ants can conquer all the Earth: if the ants can do away with their Pinkertons, if the chemical password of one ant is good with any ant on Earth, if they are compatible, if they are beloved, a trillion Davids and us their Goliaths, this miracle must be ours to copy: because if we can kill the Pinkerton then we can kill the King and Queen, and with the Pinkerton dead, even Lincoln would be safe!

Even Abraham Lincoln would be safe, if we killed the Pinkerton Detective Agency inside, the Bridge Guardian of Bridge Guardians. We must be Pontifexes all, our so many chemical technical literary cinematic bridges swarming over our miracle Earth so that there is no longer any point in guarding them.

That is a bridge you do not need to cross again. Thalossocracy, rule by sea, to democracy, rule by people, perhaps we might even do it.

I am Chumash, surrender! I am a beating heart, hear me! I Thalossocrat, I mule! I mule, cry! I am mule I cry! I cry the sea! I Pontifex Entire Rule my Mind and Body with the Breeze out from the Ocean show me your watchword primeval brother,

Chemical Brother! Show Me Your Watchword Primeval and I Our Ant Hive Mind City Grow Strong we need no gates and like Che hoped we need no borders either, except those of the Gravity Well—

Chemical Brother! I Chumash and Rat! I Salute You in the Dawn! My Name means Bright Fame Dark War, and it is a silly name implying my worth is notches on my belt, those my ancestors murdered. But perhaps not so silly. Peace is not the absence of conflict and glory is a story! Sing me a song, Chemical Brother, of the Chumash and the Angels, Mary and her Angels, stretching their strange kingdom deeper into our poor mind, reaching for the signal that we all must know—we are not alone.

We are a city under the stars!

About the Author

Robin Wyatt Dunn writes and teaches in Los Angeles. You can find him online or through email at the information below.

settdigger@gmail.com
www.robindunn.com

More books by this author

Poems from the War (forthcoming)

Conquistador of the Night Lands (forthcoming)

Julia, Skydaughter (forthcoming)

A Map of Kex's Face

Fighting Down into the Kingdom of Dreams

Line to Night Island

My Name is Dee

Los Angeles, or American Pharaohs

Performance History

A Man Stands received a staged reading at the M Street Café in Sherman Oaks, California, Thursday, Oct. 21st, 2010. Iago was read by Richard Sabine; Man was read by Octavio Velez.

About Weasel Press

Weasel Press is a new independent publisher still figuring things out in the literary world. We're dedicated in seeking quality writers and helping them get a voice in an already loud world. We're a little rusty at the moment since things are still under construction, but we hope to build a great reputation!

Our first publication was Vagabonds: Anthology of the Mad Ones. This is a literary magazine which is still printing and still growing.

This past year we've released two issues of Vagabonds partnered with Mind Steady Productions to bring an electric issue of Open Mind., moving deeper into the dark world with The Haunted Traveler.

We've got a lot of plans for the near future, so stick around and watch us grow into something awesome!

Please view our Current Publications to get a better feel for what we'll be doing in the future!

We gladly accept all questions, comments, concerns through email at:

systmaticwzl@gmail.com
http://www.weaselpress.com
http://weaselpress.storenvy.com

Made in the USA
Charleston, SC
02 November 2015